Chelsea's Psalms and Poems 3

Chelsea Kong

© 2024-2025 CHELSEA KONG

ALL RIGHTS RESERVED. ALL IMAGES USED IN THIS BOOK ARE LICENSED COPIES FROM THEIR RESPECTFUL OWNERS CANVA AND MYSELF. THIS BOOK OR ANY PORTION THEREOF MAY NOT BE REPRODUCED OR USED IN ANY MANNER WHATSOEVER WITHOUT THE EXPRESS WRITTEN PERMISSION OF THE PUBLISHER EXCEPT FOR THE USE OF BRIEF QUOTATIONS IN A BOOK REVIEW.

PRINTED IN 2024-2025, MADE IN TORONTO, CANADA
ISBN: 978-1-998335-09-1

This is written in dedication to the Lord who put it on my heart to produce this collection of psalms, poems, and songs.

The Psalms and Poems is this book are original ideas that the Lord gave to me to write and some which reference the Bible to write. I have placed them in order of when they were received.

Then on that day

Then on that day.
We will see the king of glory.
Riding on a white horse,
Clothed in robes of white dipped in blood.

The king is coming,
He is drawing near to His people.
They will see Him and be changed.

From glory to glory,
They will never be the same.
Bodies made new.
Transformed and renewed.
Incorruptible and not impossible.
He makes all things new.

September 6, 2024

Then on that day (Continued)

Faster than lightning He called us up.
All His saints are robed in white.
Riding on white horses.
A thousand years will pass away.

He will never change.
He will be the same.
He will make a way.
Justice will be done.

The righteous will win,
And He will end all sin.
On that day, He will shake the nations.

September 6, 2024

Then on that day (Continued)

He will wage war and destroy His enemies.
They will fall into the lake of fire.
For all eternity just as He said.

All people fear the Lord,
For judgement is near.
He will end all evil.

Mysteries revealed to His people.
Things yet unseen and not impossible.
Greater than our imagination.
More than what we know.

September 6, 2024

Then on that day (Continued)

Hidden in the pages of the Lord's book.
Secrets yet untold.
Things in the past and things yet to come.
Prophecies to be fulfilled.

The enemy must leave.
He will be more.
He will run and the Lord chase Him down.

He knows his time draws.
People have no fear.
For the Lord is here.

He will crush the enemy.
Underneath your feet.
They will burn for all eternity.
In the lake of fire preserved for them.

September 6, 2024

Blessings showering over me

Blessings showering over me.
Blessings from above.
The Lord releases to me.
Blessings from above.
Blessings showering with love.

A release a new anointing.
Favour, breakthrough, and wisdom.
Open doors, miracles, signs and wonders.

Supernatural power in the spirit.
Harvests so great and plentiful.
Holy Spirit breaking forth.

Revival fire the heart's desire.
Fire breaking forth.
Cleaning up my soul.

September 8, 2024

Blessings showering over me (Continued)

New wine fills me up to overflow.
Rivers of living water flowing out of me.
A new wave of the Holy Spirit arises.

Break forth and break every fetter.
My soul rejoices in the Lord.
He has changed me from the inside out.

Waves of mercy and love.
Love and compassion for the lost.
Restoration to my first love.

September 8, 2024

Blessings showering over me (Continued)

Freedom from bondage.
Now takes the focus.
Jesus as the head.

The shift has come and now its here.
Lives made new and healed.
Overcomers and sons.
The victory has been won.

A visit to the past.
A jump into the future.
Touching the present.
Changing our reality.

September 8, 2024

The Lord deserves praises

The Lord deserves the praises.
The Lord is lifted high.
He gives wisdom to the simple.

He humbles the proud.
And lifts the lowly.
The Lord is gracious and merciful.

He is altogether lovely.
Wonderful and awesome.
His power has no end.

September 8, 2024

The Lord deserves praises (Continued)

Great in mercy.
Name above every name.
Forever exalted, always.

He makes the mountains into plains.
He fills the valleys into pools of water.
He shakes the nations.

Faithful in all He does.
The Lord is just.
His kingdom never ends.

September 8, 2024

Give praise to the Lord

Give praise to the Lord.
Honour and glory belong to HIm.
He is the head of all.

God is the Maker of all the universe.
People must praise and worship Him.
Give Him worship all the heavens.

The stars in the sky sing His praise.
They give Him glory and honour Him.
Bow down before the king.

He is worthy of all praise.
Trust the Lord.
Give Him all honour and glory.

September 11, 2024

Give praise to the Lord (Continued)

He is worthy of all praise.
Favour comes from Him.
He is a worker of mysteries.

In His hands are miracles.
He is the giver of life.
Holiness is His.

The Lord lives forever.
He is eternal and the ancient of days.
He controls all creation.

September 11, 2024

Give praise to the Lord (Continued)

Trust in the Lord and lean not on your own understanding.
Raise up a standard against the enemy.

Do not give into the devil.
He is under your feet.
Jesus has crushed His head.

Faithful God who never fails you.
All things are possible with Him.
He holds you in the palm of His hands,
And you are safe.

September 11, 2024

The Lord is faithful

The Lord is faithful.
The Lord is great.
The Lord is all that we need.

In joy and in sorrow,
He is always there.
In pain and in loss,
He always comforts and heals.

He will lead you to the better place.
He will protect you always.
He is the rock on which we stand on.

Our tall tower and fortress.
A bruised reed he doesn't break.
In silence, He speaks to us.

September 12, 2024

The Lord is faithful (Continued)

Be still and know He is God.
He will answer you.
Listen and obey His instructions.

Trust in Him and you will not fail.
Hope and faith and love.
Truth and justice are His.

He avenges the righteous,
And judges the wicked,
And they are no more.

Be faithful as He is faithful.
Love righteousness and justice.
Hate evil and use self control.

September 12, 2024

The Lord is faithful (Continued)

Take hold of His Word.
Be willing and obedient,
And you will eat the good of the land.

You will have plenty.
No lack comes to you.
You will always be the head.
You won't be the tail.

Be grateful always in Him.
Love His ways, all the days of your life.

September 12, 2024

We are the work of God's hands

We are the work of God's hands.
He formed us and made us.
In the secret place, in our mother's womb.

He thought of me and made me perfect.
He knew me by name.
All my days are numbered, and my hairs counted.

There is not thought or word on my mouth
That the Lord doesn't know.
All my days are set by the Lord,
Even before I was born.

You know where I go and when I come.
You made every part.
You know me from the inside out.

September 23, 2024

We are the work of God's hands (Continued)

Everything about me is too wonderful.
It is fearfully made and beautiful.
Perfect in harmony and beauty.

Thank you, Lord for your creation.
You know it fully well.
Every path and everything is written in your book.
Even before it came to be.

You lead every step of the way every day.
Your angels guide and protect me.
Your Holy Spirit stays with me.

And I am safe under your wings.
No arrow will harm me.
No terror by night.

September 23, 2024

We are the work of God's hands (Continued)

I will rest in peace in my Maker,
He is my Father.
Jesus my Lord and Savior.
He is also my best friend and older brother.
Holy Spirit I trust in you,
My guide and teacher.
Everything I need is found in you.

September 23, 2024

Psalm 84

Lord, you dwelling place is lovely.
My soul longs to be in your courts,
My heart and flesh cry out for the living God.

The sparrow has found a home.
And she has a nest to stay in.
There she will have her young there.
It is near your altar.

Lord Almighty, you are king.
Those who live in your house are blessed.
They will always give the Lord praise.

September 24, 2024

Psalm 84 (Continued)

The Lord gives strength to those who seek Him.
They will pass through the Valley of Baka.
It will become a place of springs.

The rain from autumn covers the pools.
The Lord gives strength to His people.
They will come before the Lord in Zion.

The Lord is our sun and shield.
He gives His people favour and honour.
He gives all good things to His children,
And they walk blameless from sin.

September 24, 2024

The greatness from our God

From the east to the west, you fill my cup.
From the north to south, your word be heard.
Let it resound for every word.

There is mountain to high.
No valley to low for our God.
He controls the winds and the waves.

His voice is the still voice.
It calms the soul and heals the broken.
It makes you whole.

The Lord delivers His people from every trouble.
He shields their way and makes their paths straight.
He hears every word that comes from our mouth.

September 25, 2024

The greatness from our God (Continued)

Truth and justice will be found.
In the mouth of the righteous.
They stand solid and are not moved.

The enemy has been defeated.
He is under your feet.
There you overcome above it all.
The Lord has won and you have favour.
Let men praise the Lord!
Let them rejoice in Him!

He has given us salvation and healing.
Bind the work of the enemy.
Let be nailed to the cross
And return to the pit where it belongs.

September 25, 2024

The greatness from our God (Continued)

God's people will not be shaken.
They will not be moved.
They are covered by the blood of the Lamb.

There they stand shielded with faith.
A robe of righteousness and the armour of God.
Made holy and righteous, pure, and spotless. Amen.

September 25, 2024

The Lord causes our hands to prosper

The Lord causes our hands to prosper.
He has made the way.
He opens the door to plenty.

The heavens are open.
He pours out a blessing beyond what we can contain.
The people abound much.

Just like in Joseph's Day.
He makes our hands to succeed.
He gives us so much.

Years of plenty followed by famine.
Get wisdom and gain understanding.
In times of plenty, be wise.
Take heed and sow your seed.

September 26, 2024

The Lord causes our hands to prosper (Continued)

A mighty harvest comes.
Reap what you sow.
Give and store what you can.

Save up when there is more than enough.
Give to those in need.
And He will increase your seed.

You have more than enough.
Barns to overflow.
And so much more!

September 26, 2024

Angels

There is great rejoicing in among the angels.
Salvation is found in the Lord.
When one repents of their sins,
They greatly rejoice.

The Lord commands angels to guard you in all your ways.
To lift us up so we won't dash our foot against a stone.
They guide on the narrow path.

Thrones, powers, and authorities give way to our God.
An assembly gathers and the heaven's hosts.
They worship the Lamb who is seated on the throne.

September 28, 2024

Angels (Continued)

Millions of angels surround the throne of God.
A mighty army of them come to see His birth.
And in the end they come to fight the war.

Angel Michael leads the way
and the angels follow him.
Warriors robed in white and riding
on white horses follow the king.
Jesus Christ, the head, leads his army with victory.

Angel armies in armour fierce and strong.
Just like the army Elijah saw on the mountain top.
The same army that fought for Israel
in every battle.

September 28, 2024

Angels (Continued)

The Lord is its host.
Angels follow His command.
At His Word, they obey swift and quick.
They fly away to the places
He commands them to go.

As His servants' call,
the angels come and do their work.
They keep the God's people say.
They fight the war against their enemies and win.

September 28, 2024

Rosh Hashannah

Rejoice in the Lord!
Shout a praise to His holy name!
Blow a shofar in Zion!

Hear it on the tops of the mountains!
Jesus Christ is here!
He is king over all the land.

Awesome is His name!
The shofar will sound.
It will blast short and long,
Until the Day of the Lord comes.

September 28, 2024

Rosh Hashannah (Continued)

He will take His people up to a higher place.
They will dwell on the mountain of the Lord.
They will rejoice and be glad in Him.

He gives warning of His day.
He is coming to judge and make war.
The King of glory comes on a white horse with a sword in His hand.

A great army arises and goes forth.
To the ends of the earth, the Lord will be known.
The earth will resound with His voice.

September 28, 2024

Yom Kippur

The Lamb's blood has purchased us.
It has cleansed us from all sin.
The Lamb of God that takes away our sin.

He is Jesus Christ the Son of God and Man.
He paid the price as a sacrifice.
He bled and died to give us His life eternal.

Forever we are saved and delivered.
We are healed and restored.
He has given us more than we need.

September 28, 2024

Yom Kippur (Continued)

He atoned for our sins.
Now, we can live again.
Forever with the Lord.

He has overcome the grave.
He came to save.
And to be raised from the dead.

Resurrected with new life.
Victory and He has taken the keys.
The authority and the power.
And the dominion to rule in heaven and on earth.

September 28, 2024

Yom Kippur (Continued)

Forgiveness from within.
He cleanses us from our sin.
Sealed by His spirit and led by His Word.

Fresh bread from heaven.
Power by the Holy Spirit.
Light of the world and hidden in the secret place.
And filled with His glory.

September 28, 2024

Sukkot

Rejoice in the Lord for His promises.
Praise Him with shouts of joy!
Worship the King of glory!

He has done great things for us.
He has given us a mighty harvest.
Our homes are full of plenty.

We will not have lack.
He gives us fresh rain every season.
Due coming upon our garden leaves.

Shake the lulav with the etrog.
Wave with joy to the Lord of Hosts.
He gives showers of blessings.

September 30, 2024

Sukkot (Continued)

Take hold of them all from every direction.
North, south, east, and west.
The heavens and the earth's riches are ours.

Dance and make music to the Lord.
He has given us the promised land.
He has restored and increased us.

Great surprises are coming our way.
Miracles, signs, and wonders.
A great outpouring of the Holy Spirit.

Revival fire and our heart's desire.
Stir up the ancient wells again.
Let the glory of the Lord fill the earth.

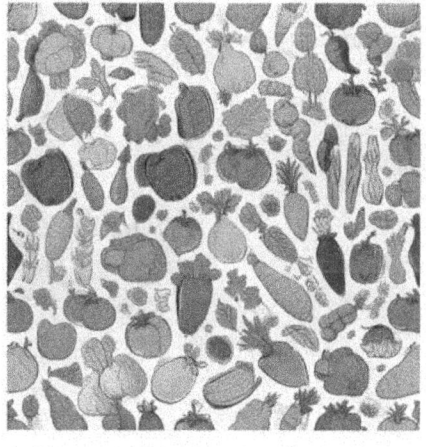

September 30, 2024

Sukkot (Continued)

The oceans and rivers,
Lakes, seas, and ponds.
Make way for the Lord!

Open the floodgates of heaven.
Pour out a blessing more than we can contain.
Harvests of souls coming into the kingdom.

Salvation, healing, and deliverance.
Breakthroughs, freedom, and more.
Open up to the Lord!

Jubilee is here.
A time of restoration and compensation.
Promises made complete.

September 30, 2024

Keep watch and pray

Open doors and so much more,
Coming to the ones He leads.
Keep secure all that is dear.

Rewards and more are coming.
The enemy will become jealous.
Keep watch and pray.

Guard all you have.
Jealous eyes are on the prize.
To seek and take you out.

They will steal, kill, and destroy all you have.
Make a plan and stay in God's hand.
Keep close to the Lord, who is your reward.

September 30, 2024

Keep watch and pray (Continued)

Secure and upgrade all you need.
Keep close and watch out for those of greed.
They trick you with simple things.

Tools of tech that are smart.
Be aware and do not assume.
They will bring you to ruin stealing all that you have.

Keep watch and pray.
It will keep the devil away.
Then you will not fear when evil draws near.

In these last days,
There is a great wave of danger.
Wicked men with a plan to come.

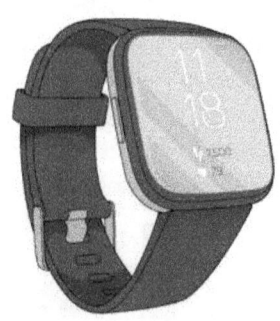

September 30, 2024

Keep watch and pray (Continued)

They seek to take all they can.
Leaving nothing left for you.
And there will be nothing you can do.

Keep watch and pray and stay away,
From public Wi-Fi sites that are not secure.
They are heists that are to lure.

And steal all you hold dear.
Tech advanced that all you have is gone.
Within seconds and all is done.

Be made aware of what is out there.
Many things are not as they seem.
Evil men can use anything to get what they want.

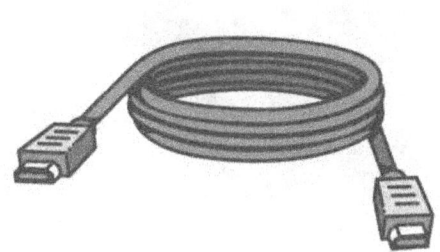

September 30, 2024

Keep watch and pray (Continued)

Be careful dear one.
Do not fall the traps.
Keep all things secure.

Keep your devices safe and locked.
Keep them near you and not open in the public.
Stay clear and not be quick in the open.

Think before you act.
Make sure not to leave anything out for anyone.
No cables, lights, and items to assume.

September 30, 2024

Keep watch and pray (Continued)

Now, many things can be used to find you out.
Dangers now everywhere of what hackers can do.
These evil men will make sure you lose.

There is nothing you can do.
Prepare yourself in advance.
Internet is not always safe to use.

Avoid cameras in your home and caution of those outside.
Anyone can hack and use them too.
They can rob all you do.

September 30, 2024

Feast of Trumpets

Make a sound on the trumpet.
Here the trumpet blast all people of God.
Rejoice and be glad!

Dance and worship and praise the Lord!
All people be glad in the Holy One of Israel.
He has saved His people.

He makes a way in the wilderness.
Rivers of living water to drink.
Out of the rock that Moses struck.

The Lord shows mercy and His lovingkindness.
To all generations, they will know His faithfulness.
He makes a highway in the wilderness.

October 3, 2024

Feast of Trumpets (Continued)

He split the Red Sea and made the way.
A pillar of cloud by day.
And a pillar of fire by night.

He stopped the Egyptians and Pharaoh.
They are no more.
All of them have drowned in the sea.
A new year has come.
A year to thank the Lord for miracles.
Signs and wonders man has never known.

Come before His tabernacle.
Seek His face and know His glory.
In the secret place, He speaks.

October 3, 2024

Feast of Trumpets (Continued)

He makes known mysteries.
He shares ideas and plans.
He tells secrets to His people.

The old has passed away.
The new has come.
A new beginning for everyone!

October 3, 2024

Day of Atonement

Prepare yourself and household.
Gather and remove every yeast.
Be clean and your house too.

Remove every sin that holds you down.
Repent before the Lord.
Give Him all honour and glory.

Fear the Lord in honouring Him.
Seek His face and receive Him.
The blood of the Lamb has made us whole.

Let your will be in His control.
He is the God He leads the way.
Mend our hearts and help us to stay.

October 10, 2024

Day of Atonement (Continued)

Take God's Word to heart.
Let it be there from the start.
The beginning and the end.

That's the plan to set the captives free.
That we believe in Him.
And accept Jesus Christ.
The Son of God's sacrifice.
He gives us a new life.
And everything that we need.

Keep close to Him
And you will never leave.
He will be your safeguard.

October 10, 2024

Day of Atonement (Continued)

The devil has a plan.
To take you away in his plan.
He will lead you astray.

Then you will lose your way.
Without God in your heart.
You will fall apart.

Do not let shame, guilt, and pain.
Come upon your name.
Be free and see the truth, life, and the way.

He breaks the shackles that bind you.
He gives you hope, peace, and joy.
Freedom, grace, and mercy.

October 10, 2024

Day of Atonement (Continued)

Everything transgression and iniquity.
He has removed it from you,
When you took on the name of His Son.

He is the only One who saves, heals, and delivers.
He knows what to do.
He will always be with you.

No matter what happens.
He is always there to help you everywhere you go.
Angels watching and guarding.

October 10, 2024

Day of Atonement (Continued)

Taking you in the narrow way.
You will give thanks and praise.
Give glory to His name.

It's a new day.
A new year to start again.
New and forgiven.

Fast and pray and seek His way.
Read and receive all that you need.
Believe and grow and hear His voice.

Holy Spirit, lead and guide you.
Fill you and overflow.
That's the way to go.

October 10, 2024

Thanksgiving

Be thankful to the Lord all the time.
Let praise always be in your mouth.
Set your hearts to be glad.

Rejoice in the Lord! He has made all things.
And count the blessings.

The Lord has done great things.
We are blessed.
Favour, health, food, and gifts come from Him.

He gives all we need and more.
There is so much in store for you,
Beyond our imagination.

October 10, 2024

Thanksgiving (Continued)

Be thankful every day.
Be thankful in every way.
Be thankful for all you do.

God is with you.
The big and the small.
He has given them all.
A time to share and time to care.
Family, home, and school.
Church, work, and fun too.

Finance, wealth, and government.
Sports, health, and games.
Movies, media, law.

October 10, 2024

Thanksgiving (Continued)

He has made them all!
From the greatest to the least.
Wisdom, honour, and glory.

Rewards to those who follow Him.
The best of everything.
And they prosper in all they do.

It is all because of only you, the Lord.
He has made us, and we are His.
No matter what you do.

Do not forget the Lord and be grateful to.
Thanksgiving is a praise to Him.
He that has given everything.

October 10, 2024

Song of Thanksgiving

With joy, we praise you.
Remember the good things the Lord has done.
The blessings we have received.

In morning and afternoon,
In evening and evening,
Give thanks to the Lord!

Worship, dance, and sing,
Before the Holy King.
He gives us everything that we need.

October 13, 2024

Song of Thanksgiving (Continued)

He will pour even more into those who believe.
They shall receive abundantly.
More than what they need to give to others.

He has forgiven us and given us eternal life.
We are free and new in Christ Jesus.
He has washed away our sins.

Our transgressions and iniquities are gone.
We hide in the secret place of the Highest God.
He has covered us with His feathers.

October 13, 2024

Song of Thanksgiving (Continued)

He has atoned for our sins.
Through Christ Jesus, the perfect sacrifice.
He has paid the price.

All sickness and disease must leave.
At the sound of His voice.
They must bow before the Lord Almighty.
Give us this day our daily bread.
Forgive us for all trespasses,
As we forgive those who sinned against us.

October 13, 2024

Song of Thanksgiving (Continued)

Lead us not into temptation,
But deliver us from evil.
Yours is the Kingdom and power and the glory forever. Amen.

Give thanks and praise to the Ancient of Days!
Rejoice in the King of kings and Lord of lords.
Forever and always. Amen.

October 13, 2024

Thanksgiving Day

Give thanks every day.
In every season and every moment.
Remember all His blessings and benefits.

Do not forget the Lord when things are good.
Count the blessings He has given.
Thank Him for each one.

In times of trouble, give thanks to the Lord.
Every place that you go, give thanks to the Lord.
When you are alone and with others, give thanks to Him.

October 14, 2024

Thanksgiving Day

Celebrate with gladness and a thankful heart.
Remember His promises and name each one.
Keep a record of them to remember.

Do not forget the good things He has done.
The Lord gives the best to everyone who is His.
And favour rests on them.

Delight in the Lord, always.
And He will give you the desires of your heart.
And so much more than you ask for and imagine.

October 14, 2024

Feast of Tabernacles (Sukkot)

Rejoice in the Lord and His promises.
He redeemed us from sin.
He made a way for us.

Praise to the Lord and welcome Him in.
He has washed away our sin.
We have let Him come in.

Let us build booths to live in.
Feast and worship Him.
Give thanks and receive from Him.

Ask Him for His blessings.
From the east, west, north, and south.
Blessings from heaven and the earth.

October 18, 2024

Feast of Tabernacles (Sukkot)

Showers of rain falling from above.
More than enough to satisfy us.
Holy Spirit let your power pour on us.

A fresh anointing rising from within.
A new flame and wind.
Empower your people to rise again,

Revival fires and no dead flames.
Burning up within our frame.
Tongues of fire dancing on our heads.

October 18, 2024

Feast of Tabernacles (Sukkot)

Words unknown from our tongues.
Rivers from our belly.
A great joy that was never known.

Like the apostles, we have been called.
To walk in the spirit of the Lord.
Making disciples and baptising them in His name.

That is the reason that He came to save us.
That we will live eternally for His glory.
A beautiful bride beyond history, time and space.

October 18, 2024

New Creation and the Lord's return

A new heaven and new earth.
Welcomes us home.
Up and away, we go!

When the time comes, only those in God will know.
Gone from this world.
The Lord will come to make Himself known.

Then all humankind will know.
He is the Holy One.
And those who are not with Him fear and run!

October 18, 2024

New Creation and the Lord's return (Continued)

To those who are His.
Peace and joy will come.
Forever with the king they will be.

No more sorrow, pain, or suffering.
Only good things for the old have gone and the new has come.
The new order of God's kingdom comes.

October 18, 2024

Sukkot

The lives in the Tabernacle.
Jesus Christ the Living One.
He lives with us.

Living in the heart of man.
This is God's plan.
To remember the promise in Exodus.

Wave the palm leaves and the myrtle branches.
And hold the etrog in your hand.
Honour the Lord of the harvest.

October 18, 2024

New Creation and the Lord's return (Continued)

The priest taking the water.
Pours the sacrifice.
On the 8th day is the greatest day of the feast.

The Lord has blessed us with rain.
Plenty has been given.
The Lord says come thirsty and drink.

The Living One that is God's Son.
Opens the eyes of the blind.
He brings healing in His name.
.
The Light of the world for all people.
He has come to light the way.
And He is always here every day.

October 18, 2024

Celebration to the Lord

Take an offering before the Lord.
Worship at His feet.
Honour Him in His presence daily.

Lift and wave the lulav and etrog.
Wave to the east, south, west, and the north.
Wave to the heavens and the earth.

Receive God's blessings all year round.
Open doors of blessings from heaven above.
Come to those who are filled of love.

Faith and miracles,
Signs and wonders.
Peace, joy, and freedom in His name.

October 22, 2024

Celebration to the Lord (Continued)

Salvation, healing, breakthroughs!
Dance, praise, worship, and sing.
Play the instruments to the Holy king.

Rejoice and be glad in Him!
Rejoice and be glad in Him!
Glory, glory, glory to the Holy One.
He sits on the throne.
Awesome in power and majesty.
Gracious, merciful, and faithful.

Stay in His presence of the Lord.
Wait on Him and seek His face.
Give Him first place always.

October 22, 2024

Wonder of God's Creation

How wonderful is God's creation.
So full of colour and of life.
Vibrant and flowing.

Great are the winds and the waves of the oceans.
The storms and all the seas.
The mountains so awesome and beautiful.

The lakes, hills, and flowers so lovely.
Calm are the streams and rivers of water.
That the animals drink of it daily.

The fields so quiet and vast.
That the sheep lay in its meadows.
Peaceful rest comes to them who trust in the Lord.

October 22, 2024

Wonder of God's Creation (Continued)

You will be planted by the water.
Those who rest in the Lord will have peace and joy.
They will be filled with life and abundance forever.

Nothing will bother those who are whole.
They will have great victory.
Their life so free and strong in faith.

The sun, moon, and stars shine their light.
The Northern lights their beautiful array.
Into the night their lights are bright.

October 22, 2024

Wonder of God's Creation (Continued)

In summer the sun is like a blazing fire.
The waters so comforting to those who swim in them.
The fish and the creatures enjoy its cool temperatures.

Nature is a joy to the soul.
It refreshes the weary soul and brings good things.
It's beauty beyond compare.

Unforgettable memories that people find.
And never enough to satisfy the mind,
Making them want more time away from their busy life.

October 22, 2024

Prophetic Vision

Stand and look to see a vision.
Hear the voice of the Lord.
The audible voice of the Lord.

He tells of the future yet to come.
In a still small voice, He also speaks.
He shares mysteries that we don't know.

The Spirit of the Lord dwells among His people.
He gives them power and authority.
They seek, hear, and obey the Lord.

The Lord instructs His people where to go.
There they find pasture and peace.
Direction and provision are theirs.

October 22, 2024

Prophetic Vision (Continued)

Eyes like the eagle to see far and wide.
They soar to heights like eagles upon the wind.
Their faith and their senses are strong.

A vision by day and a dream at night.
A word of the Lord bursting out of their belly.
Rivers of living water overflows.

Wells of revival awaken.
The Holy Spirit is in motion.
People getting set free and being saved.

October 22, 2024

I will rise

I will rejoice and be glad.
Soar like the eagle.
In Jesus' name, no longer bound by Satan.

I will rise with eagle wings.
I will soar, and I will rise with freedom.
Victory and I will be free.

I will rise on eagle's wings.
I will rise, I will rise, I will rise.
I will rise in the Lord.

I will rise, and I will soar!
I will rise and take my place.
The solid rock Jesus Christ He reigns.

November 7, 2024

I will rise (Continued)

I will rise upon this rock.
I will soar to the highest mountain in the Lord.
He's my refuge and my fortress.

You are the only one I need.
You alone are worthy.
Jesus Christ, you are everything.
I need you more than anything, Lord.
Change my heart.
Let your fire burn and remove all the dross.

November 7, 2024

I will rise (Continued)

Restore me.
You make me new, my king.
You alone are the solid rock.

God will restore and renew our hearts.
I trust in you alone.
You are my refuge and my victory.

You are my strength in time of need.
You are everything that I need.
Revive me again.

November 7, 2024

Rising in the Lord

Lord, I need you more than anything.
I will rise with your strength.
Wholehearted I will worship.

Let your anointing flow in me.
That I would have the heart to see the way you do.
Let me have the passion, Lord.

The Holy Spirit burn in me again.
Awaken my soul.
Let me be refreshed by your Holy Spirit.

November 7, 2024

Rising in the Lord (Continued)

I love you, Jesus.
There is none like you.
Lord, heal me and strengthen me.

Let me have the mind of Christ in you.
Let me worship you in all I do.
That my heart will rejoice in you.

November 7, 2024

Return to the Lord all people

Return to the Lord all people.
Return to the King of Kings.
Repent of your sins, all people.

He has brought us out of judgement.
He has raised us up.
He has brought freedom to this land.

Victory is in His hand.
He has heard the cry of His people.
And He answered and chose mercy.

November 8, 2024

Return to the Lord all people (Continued)

He raised up a man and called him.
He made him to be a trumpet to sound the alarm.
To awaken the nations to return to their God.

A man like Jehu that was chosen to bring justice.
Used by the Lord to bring judgement to the wicked.
A man of war and man that honoured the Lord.

Raise up a banner and shout to the King of Kings.
Great is the Holy One of Israel.
He has won and will restore.

November 8, 2024

Return to the Lord all people (Continued)

The land will become abundant again.
It will produce great wealth, riches, and fruit again.
Great will be the revival that comes to that nation.

Those who fear God will overcome.
They will have outstanding success and rise.
The Lord increases those who are His.

They will greatly rejoice in His goodness.
His righteousness rules in the land.
Once again, the Lord will rule this nation.

November 8, 2024

Return to the Lord all people (Continued)

Fear the Lord and hate evil.
Let justice be done and the wicked be removed.
They will be found no more.

The Lord will destroy those who hate him.
He will strip them of their power and authority.
He will put them to shame.

November 8, 2024

A great war in heaven

A war in heaven is heard.
One that no angel has known.
Lucifer became proud.

The elders and the four living creatures become quiet.
Opening the way for God to show His light.
The Mighty and holy one knows all so well.

God has allowed a lesson to be learned.
Nothing is a surprise to Him.
The one who became full of sin.

November 8, 2024

A great war in heaven

Losing all beauty, power, and authority that God gave.
Now, ugly and black and full of rage.
Blood red and full of evil, he mocks God and His angels.

Angel Michael and Gabriel come forth.
Ready to war against Lucifer and his fallen angels.
A mighty battle among the angels.

Fell down from heaven, Lucifer goes.
At the sound of God's son,
He says, "Depart from me."

November 8, 2024

A great war in heaven (Continued)

Into the darkness,
Lucifer has fallen.
No more in beauty and splendour.

Out of jealousy, he comes to steal, kill, and destroy.
With a new name, he comes.
Satan is the evil one.

Before the end comes, the nations will rage war.
Upon and against Israel, they come.
To destroy and take from God's people.

November 8, 2024

A great war in heaven (Continued)

A time is coming and will be here for Jesus the Christ to rule here.
A battle on earth of heavenly hosts.
The final judgement of God.

In the end, they will not win.
God, Jesus Christ, and the army will come.
They will put an end to the evil one.

The fallen angels and Satan will be no more.
A new heaven and a new earth will come.
A time of glory for everyone in God's kingdom

November 8, 2024

Remember the Lord

Remember the Lord and return to your first love.
It is He that has made us and not ourselves.
Hear His voice and follow His word.

The Lord has chosen you to be a holy people.
Set part for His purpose and glory.
Give Him what He deserves.

The Lord calls to His people.
Come and seek my face.
Pray and repent of your sins.

Be washed in the blood of the lamb.
Wait on Him and renew your strength.
Rise and soar as the eagle.

November 10, 2024

Remember the Lord (Continued)

Take authority over the enemy.
Do not fear and do not be dismayed.
Honour the Lord and worship Him only.

Behold the Lord in the beauty of His majesty.
Be in awe of His greatness.
Exalt His holy name.
The nations will come before Him.
They will bow down and worship Him.
They will bring their crowns and lay them at His feet.

November 10, 2024

Remember the Lord (Continued)

The Lord is a mighty warrior.
He fights for Israel and He will win.
He will destroy all enemies.

The wicked will fall and be gone.
They will be put to shame.
Their life will be cut short.

All that the wicked have stored
The Lord will take away
And give to the righteous.

November 10, 2024

Remember the Lord (Continued)

His glory will be known in all the earth.
Revival to the nations and salvation.
Blessings and fruitfulness to the land.

Rejoice and be glad for the Lord!
He is the one that has blessed you with plenty.
More than you need.

Hear the voice of the Lord.
Obey and do as He say.
And you will be rewarded.

November 2024

Remember the Lord (Continued)

Honour your father and mother.
Then you will live long.
And have a good life.

Be aware of those jealous of you.
Watch and pray and do not fall into their traps.
Keep your heart in the Lord and speak only His Word.

November 2024

Jehovah Jireh

Jehovah Jireh is my provider.
Through the times of trouble.
You can count on Him.

The economy will rise and fall,
But the Lord is forever stable.
And is your rock and source of supply.

No matter what happens around you.
He will always provide for you.
He is faithful and He will never change.

November 15, 2024

Jehovah Jireh (Continued)

The Lord is gracious and merciful,
Compassionate to thousands of generations.
Forgiving and loving.

He knows your every need.
He cares for you in every season.
He watches and waits.

His time is perfect and in it comes blessings.
Favour and goodness will follow.
He will give you more than what you need.

November 15, 2024

Jehovah Jireh (Continued)

He reveals the hidden treasures and gives it to His own.
They will never have lack.
He will always give more than what you deserve.

Wealth is coming to His people.
Wealth beyond your expectations.
You will be abundant and fruitful.

Those who trust in the Lord are blessed.
They are saved from trouble.
They will always be the head and not the tail.

November 15, 2024

Jehovah Jireh (Continued)

Riches will follow the righteous.
The Lord has plenty and gives it to His own.
The wealth of the wicked is stored up for the righteous.

The wicked will see it no more.
Those who are righteous will continue to prosper.
All the days of their life they increase.

The Lord grants wisdom, knowledge, and understanding.
They have great success and will rule the land.
Nations will give to the Lord and kneel at his feet.

November 15, 2024

Jehovah Jireh (Continued)

The righteous will never go hungry or beg for bread.
They will be loved and cared for.
They will be exalted to a high place.

There worries, fears, and losses will be gone.
They will grow strong roots and rise.
They will be bold and give God glory.

On eagle's wings, they will soar.
They will be renewed with strength.
They will see with great vision.

Their enemies will become prey for them.
They trample them under their feet.
They feed on God's word and are full.

November 15, 2024

Seek the Lord

Seek the Lord in the morning and at night.
Seek Him in the afternoon and the evening.
Seek the Lord all the time.

He is your very great reward.
Look to Him in all you do.
Pray and wait on Him.

Hear the Lord speak.
Meditate on His Word.
Build yourself in the Holy Spirit.

November 15, 2024

Seek the Lord (Continued)

Rest in the beauty of His holiness.
Great and awesome are His deeds.
And God's counsel is wise.

Be still and know that the Lord is good.
He is remembered for generations.
Say His Word and you will prosper.

November 15, 2024

Faithful

The Lord is faithful in all He does.
He will never leave you nor forsake you.
He will always be near you.

No matter where you go or who you are with.
The Lord will always be there.
He is watching and waiting.

He is Jehovah Shammah.
The Lord is there.
He keeps you on the straight and narrow path.

November 18, 2024

Faithful (Continued)

He is there when you call on His name.
The Lord is faithful and true.
He will always remember you.

In times of trouble, call on His name.
In time of sorrow, He is your peace.
In the good times, He is the one that blesses you.

His mercy never runs out.
His faithfulness lasts to thousands of generations.
He will give you new life and hope.

November 18, 2024

Faithful (Continued)

He is your counsel and help in time of need.
He keeps you in line with His truth.
And when you go astray, He will come to lead the way.

Give thanks and praise to the Lord.
He is faithful in all He does.
He will take you on solid ground.

November 18, 2024

Return to the Lord

Return to the Lord, your Maker.
It's time to repent and to start new again.
It's time to return to your first love.

The Lord is watching and waiting.
He knows your ways and deeds.
Nothing's hidden from Him.

In whatever you do and wherever you go,
He is there with you.
He is before you and behind you.

The wicked will fall.
The righteous will rise again.
They will soar on eagle's wings.

December 1, 2024

Return to the Lord (Continued)

Anointed of the Lord return to Him.
Do not mingle and do not stay with the wicked.
Run to the Lord quickly while there is still time.

The days are coming, says the Lord.
The wicked are judged.
The righteous will stand and have victory.
The Lord calls to His people.
They hear His voice and will not follow the stranger.
They will return to the Lord.

The days are coming
when great evil will come to world.
Many's hearts will grow cold.
Many fall into the world's ways.

December 1, 2024

Return to the Lord (Continued)

Many fall into buying and selling into the new order.
They will fall and fall hard.
They will not return from it.

Those who are God's remain faithful in Him.
Trust in the Lord is always in the end.
He is your provider and will deliver you.

The righteous will hide in the Lord and be safe.
Learn and live while you can and do great things.
A time is coming and almost here where things will turn around.

December 1, 2024

Return to the Lord (Continued)

Great evil is coming to this world.
And yet there will be peace among
those who belong to God.
They will find rest in Him.

Be aware, watch and pray for
you don't know the hour He comes.
The Lord has set the times and seasons.
He warns His people ahead of time.

The Lord instructions and saves them.
He keeps them in the days of evil.
He will take them with Him.

December 1, 2024

Return to the Lord (Continued)

There is so much to do and so little time.
Obey the Lord as He leads.
Do not hear another's voice.

All the other voices are wicked.
They will lead you astray.
Family and friends will turn on you

But the Lord is faithful.
Those who are in the Lord will stay true.
They will be with you in the end.

Still, the Lord is your anchor.
He is the one you must trust and rely on.
Nobody will be there to help you except the Lord.

December 1, 2024

Families

The Lord loves families.
He puts singles in families.
They are blessing from Him.

United, they stand and overcome.
Together, they destroy the enemy,
Underneath their feet.

Great is the authority in their house.
A wise woman builds her house.
She makes her house strong.

December 1, 2024

Families (Continued)

Through her words, she gives praise and thanks.
She encourages and comforts.
She reminds them of God's love.

A man who is in charge is blessed,
When he obeys the Lord.
His wife praises him.

A man who is blessed is like a tree planted.
His leaves are green, and water is plenty.
He lies down by green pasture and is safe.

December 1, 2024

Families (Continued)

His children are blessed and give praise.
All that they do is be a blessing from the Lord.
The Lord will exalt them.

Families that are blessed by the Lord are rewarded.
Great is the joy and favour in their lives.
The Lord protects them from evil.

He exalts them and promotes them above their peers.
He gives them more than enough.
They succeed in all that they do.

They live in peace.
Their home is blessed and everything they own.
They can give freely without fear.

December 1, 2024

Families (Continued)

The Lord gives them perfect health and expands their land.
He increases all that they own.
He gives them the best.

Everywhere they go, goodness and mercy follow them.
They have wisdom and understanding.
They take care of others in need.

They show love and are generous.
They keep their house clean of evil.
They pray and seek the Lord always.

December 1, 2024

Blessings

Come before the Lord with thanksgiving and praise.
Shout for joy for His goodness.
Give thanks for all He has done.

Abundance comes on the righteous.
Blessings from above showers on them.
Behold, the Lord is the Blesser and Jesus is the Blessing.

Blessed are those who obey the Lord.
They will be remembered and have a place in Him.
They will rejoice always and be glad.

December 5, 2024

Blessings (Continued)

Remember what the Lord has done.
Do not forget Him who has made you.
He is your rock and refuge in good times and in danger.

The righteous have favour.
The wicked will fall away.
The Lord judges all and gives mercy to the righteous.

The Lord judges the wicked and He will win.
He will never forget the righteous.
The evil he will punish and be destroyed.

December 5, 2024

Blessings (Continued)

Blessings will follow the righteous all the days of their life.
They will see the Lord in days to come.
Even when the world is in want, the Lord will provide for His people.

The righteous will live long, and He will take them with Him.
They will be seen no more by the wicked.
The righteous will be with the Lord forever.

December 5, 2024

Ottawa and Canada

The Lord will rule again in Ottawa.
The Lord rules over the nation of Canada.
Where pools of water and refreshing
And healing streams will flow.

Canada will shine from sea to shining sea.
Fire like lava shall burn.
The power of the Holy Spirit upon the nation.

People shall rise and worship the king.
The land of plenty and the breadbasket of the world.
Sending missionaries to the various parts of the world.

December 8, 2024

Ottawa and Canada (Continued)

The Lord is king over Canada.
Canada shall arise and bring glory to the Lord.
There is none like the Lord God Almighty.

He will exalt the lowly and tear down the proud.
He restores the weak and provides for the needy.
None shall go hungry and thirsty again.

Praise the Lord and give thanks to Him.
He is your Provider through all situations.
Look to the Lord always and you will never lack.

Through the trials and tribulations,
He will always be there.
He will make a way for you.

December 8, 2024

Ottawa and Canada (Continued)

Rejoice and be glad in the Lord.
People rejoice for the Lord will redeem you.
And He will keep you to the end.

Toronto is His meeting place.
A city chosen by the Lord to bring revival.
Return to the Lord who is your first love.

Remember Him because He made you.
You are His chosen vessels for divine purpose.
For many will come to the Lord through you.
The Lord's plan shall be established on the earth
As it is in heaven.

December 8, 2024

Festival of Lights

Jesus the light of the world.
The brightest light for all to see.
The salt of the earth.

A time of dedication and celebration.
The festival of lights is here.
Remember the one who gives life eternal.

His sheep hear His voice and they know Him.
They follow after Him all their days.
They will never follow a stranger.

December 18, 2024

Festival of Lights (Continued)

The Lord has given His people hope in times of darkness.
He has made the light.
He has opened the way for them.

A miracle has come to God's people.
They once were defeated but now overcome.
The Lord reminds them of their past.

Victory came from the Lord.
The people fought and won.
Eight days after the menorah was lit.

December 18, 2024

Festival of Lights (Continued)

The Lord has kept it going.
It will not go out day or night.
It stays strong and bright.

December 18, 2024

The greatest gift

A time to give and a time to praise.
A time of thanks and a time of grace.
A time for love and a time for joy.

Remembering the reason for the season.
It's not to focus on receiving gifts
But to celebrate the goodness of God.

The greatest gift of all.
A miracle born to a virgin by the Holy Spirit.
Wrapped in light.

God's only Son sent to earth
To save us from our sins.
A heavy price that we should think twice.

December 26, 2024

The greatest gift (Continued)

How blessed we are to have His sacrifice.
No other can redeem man from sin
But only the Son of God and Son of Man.

Eternal life for all who believe.
Earth will fade away and be no more
God's throne will remain forever.

In the time that lambs are born,
God's Son came as a lamb.
He was spotless and without sin.

December 26, 2024

The greatest gift

He was crucified for our sin.
Crushed and persecuted.
Then raised up and given a new life.

And in the time of Herod's census
Joseph and Mary went to Bethlehem.
This fulfilled God's plan.

Look into the past and see at last.
The true time of Jesus' birth.
It is not what most think.

December 26, 2024

The greatest gift (Continued)

Deception comes to man who don't know God's plan.
They make a lie that they teach and claim as truth.
For the Bible does say, that Jesus was born on Christmas Day.

Evil loves to deceive and make one believe
The wrong things so that others will never know.
There are those who seek to find the truth and discover it.

Many will never know.
God says, "Seek and you will find,
Knock and the door will be open to you."

December 26, 2024

Seeking Jesus

Seek the Lord and He will be found.
Knock and the door will be opened to you.
Open the door of your heart and believe.
Receive the Savior and the Lord of Lords.

The shepherds did see the Lord as a child
With their sheep and lambs, they came.
Born at night, the star shone so brightly.
Behold, the Savior is born!

Sheep are not born in winter but in spring, summer, and fall.
In the height of the time of feasts, the people gather.
Traveling from one place to another.
They celebrate the high holy days of the Lord.

December 28, 2024

Seeking Jesus (Continued)

The scriptures tell the truth
That Jesus was not born on Christmas Day.
For man doesn't normally travel on cold winter
days and nights.
Nor do they enjoy the rainy weather.

Sheep are kept indoors on cold winter days.
Never do they stay outside in the winter months.
Hanukkah is not a bible feast but only a holiday.
That families can gather in their homes.

To celebrate and remember the past
and what the Lord has done.
Families tell stories, sing, play games,
eat, and give gifts.
They keep the menorah lit each night.
Then they light another candle for every night.

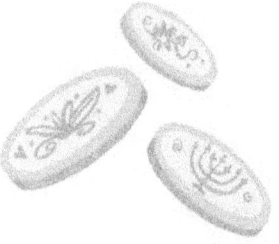

December 28, 2024

Seeking Jesus (Continued)

For the Magi sought the Lord as they followed the star.
For there were more than three magi with many soldiers.
They sought the Lord and found him after some time passed.
No longer a baby but a child and at the house of Joseph.

Do not always believe what the world says.
As they do not know what is written in the word.
In truth, Christmas is a pagan holiday in history.
Chosen by man to celebrate Jesus' birth.

December 28, 2024

Seeking Jesus (Continued)

The symbols like the tree, the lights, presents, and more.
These all come from cultures that celebrate other things.
Not everyone will believe until they read the articles online.
Man deceives many to accept a lie and nobody argues against it.

Even the time of year of Jesus' birth was missed.
The Western calendar itself is another misleading tool.
The Hebrew calendar is closer to the truth.

December 28, 2024

Seeking Jesus (Continued)

Many will not want to believe.
For many hate the Jews.
They refuse to seek the truth.
Rome chose their choice on what they wanted.
They made it public for all to know.

Seek the Lord and He will show you what you need to know.
Many will hate to know the truth and will not find it.
They will look, and it will not be given.
Only those with genuine hearts can receive.

December 28, 2024

Seeking Jesus (Continued)

There are many who argue.
Ask the Jesus and He will tell you.
Nothing should be mixed with other cultures and traditions.
The Lord has spoken against in His Word.

He will spit out the lukewarm and the cold.
The hot will remain in the Lord and must stay hot.
The Lord doesn't like a lukewarm or cold believer.
The Lord doesn't like mixture with anything not in His Word.

He detests man's traditions that aren't His ways.
Jesus Christ is your direct connection to God.
There is no other way.

December 28, 2024

New Beginnings

It's a new season.
A new year has come.
Make a choice for the Lord.
That He is the first for everyone.

A new year to fast and pray.
A new year to start in a new way.
To turn to the Lord and hear what He has to say.

Follow and obey every day.
It's a time for a man to choose wisely
Which way he will go.

A fresh start and a new beginning.
For all of our days we should give God praise.
Our years to worship Him.

January 1, 2025

New Beginnings (Continued)

His plan is the best, so we will not stress.
Good things will come to everyone who follows the Son.
Leave the past behind and start on time.

Walk by faith and not by sight.
New opportunities and doors will open.
Freedom and breakthroughs will come.

Families and reunions.
Unity and revival.
The Lord makes His presence known.

January 1, 2025

New Beginnings (Continued)

?Then the nations will know He is God.
Each day you will find a new way
To give Him glory.

Great rewards are in store.
Great plans to be revealed.
Take the path of faith and receive it.

January 1, 2025

The Lord blesses

The Lord blesses the righteous.
Those who are poor and needy
He provides for them and gives them families.

The Lord turns the wilderness into a pool of water.
He makes the dry into water springs.
He brings to those who are His.

The hungry will dwell and prepare a city for habitation.
They will sow fields and plant vineyards.
They will see its fruit grow and increase.

January 6, 2025

The Lord blesses (Continued)

He blesses and multiples them greatly.
He keeps their animals from decreasing.
The upright people are glad, and they are clean.

All people will praise the Lord for His goodness.
They will praise Him for His loving-kindness.
They will give glory to His wonderful works.

The Lord will be blessed and exalted.
He is a great God, and His name lasts forever.
He blesses the righteous and gives them more.

They will be forever grateful.
His kingdom lasts forever
And His favour lasts a lifetime.

January 6, 2025

Praise the Lord in all circumstances

Praise the Lord in all circumstances.
Praise Him in all situations.
Know that He is God.

Through the good and the bad.
Honour Him all the time and always.
He is the first and the last.

Overcome anger and negative feelings
With the power of God's word and praise.
Be thankful all the time.

January 8, 2025

Praise the Lord in all circumstances (Continued)

Keep your eyes on Jesus through it all.
He will give you victory to rise above them.
Let the joy of the Lord be your strength.

Keep a song in your heart and faith in your words.
Speak His promises and remember His goodness.
Keep the word in your heart, mind, and feelings.

Rejoice in the Lord always.
Meditate on the Word of God always.
Come before His presence with thanksgiving.

January 8, 2025

The Lord blesses the righteous

The Lord blesses the house of the righteous.
He gives them plenty so they will not beg for bread.
Their cup will overflow abundantly.

The Lord gives them favour.
He opens the way for them.
The wicked stumble and fall into a pit.

The righteous stand and are saved.
God protects those who are His.
He sends His angels to protect them, and they are safe.

January 10, 2025

The Lord blesses the righteous (Continued)

The Lord causes their enemies to fall.
He turns them around so they can't be found.
The prepares a banquet for His people before their enemies.

He will drive all their enemies out.
He will bring confusion among them.
He will complete a good work in and through His people.

All the Lord has promised He will fulfill.
No weapon formed against His people will stand.
They will arise above their enemies.

January 10, 2025

The Lord blesses the righteous (Continued)

They are more than conquerors through Christ Jesus.
Success is in their hands.
Favour and blessing are theirs.

The house of the righteous is a strong tower.
It's based a firm foundation.
No evil will come against it for the Lord has blessed it.

Thank you, Lord Almighty.
Great is your name and worthy of all praise.
Let the earth bring you all honour and glory forever. Amen.

January 10, 2025

Be Holy

The Lord is holy and those who belong to Him must be holy.
Be holy in all you do.
The word says, "Be holy, because I am holy."

The fear of the Lord is the beginning of wisdom.
The Lord will guide you in holiness.
He will change ashes for beauty.

As you surrender to Him, you will be changed.
Purity and holiness will be your life.
Your words will become sweet as honey.

January 10, 2025

Be Holy (Continued)

**The joy of the Lord is your strength.
You will become wise in all you do.
You will enjoy a long life.**

**The Lord hates sin, but he loves the righteous.
He gives them freedom from their sin.
And they are saved and overcome.**

January 10, 2025

Breakthroughs

The Lord is the master of breakthroughs.
He is the Baal-Perazim.
Jehovah Sabaoth, the Lord of Hosts.

The Lord of angel armies.
He fights and wages war.
The Lord our God who watches over us.

He is always there for you all the time.
The Lord is our victor and a mighty God.
He overcomes and gives us victory.

January 18, 2025

Breakthroughs (Continued)

The Lord is our shield and buckler.
He is our strong tower and very present help in time of need.
He is our defender and protector.

He is our sword against the enemy.
No weapon formed against us will prosper.
No enemy will stand.

We will take on a thousand.
Two of us will take on ten thousand.
The Lord is with us and will excel.

January 18, 2025

The Seven-fold Spirit of God

Trust in the Lord and His Seven-fold Spirit.
The Spirit of the Lord.
He is the Spirit of wisdom.
The Spirit of understanding.

The Spirit of counsel.
The Spirit of power.
The Spirit of knowledge.
And the Spirit of the fear of the Lord.

January 18, 2025

The Seven-fold Spirit of God (Continued)

And by His Holy Spirit, we are made perfect.
He is mighty in power and mighty to save.
Mighty to heal, restore, and bless.
Mighty in battle and mighty in authority.

The earth will see Him and know He is God.
The heavens will praise Him.
The people who believe will rejoice.
The wicked will fall before Him and be judged.

January 18, 2025

The Lord is gracious and merciful

The Lord is gracious and merciful.
The Lord is all knowing and powerful.
He moves with His might.

No man knows where the wind goes.
They see how it moves things around
But they don't see it.

They hear the sound of the wind.
They don't know what it will do next.
The Lord knows and sees all things.

The Lord causes the wind to blow.
He makes it move over the waters.
He makes it move over the land and in the air.

January 25, 2025

The Lord is gracious and merciful (Continued)

He is in charge of the new year and the seasons.
He blesses those He chooses.
He takes away from those who are against Him.

He blesses the righteous, but judges the wicked.
He teaches His people but allows suffering for sin.
He delights in the righteous as they seek Him.

Spring, summer, fall, and winter are in His hands.
All man's plans will fail, but the Lord's plans will never fail.
He will make it happen in His time.

January 25, 2025

The Lord is gracious and merciful (Continued)

Blessed are those who obey the Lord.
They will have no lack and want.
All things come to them and more than what they need.

They overflow with plenty and are kind to others.
They have love for others and care for the needy.
They listen to the Lord, and they are rewarded.

January 25, 2025

God's Love

God's love is deep, far, and wide.
No matter where you go, it will never leave you.
It lasts forever and a lifetime.

God's love never fails.
He sent Christ to die for us.
He loved the world and gave His only Son.

Through Jesus, we have eternal life.
God is love and whoever abides in love abides in God.
He also abides in him.

February 8, 2025

God's Love (Continued)

God is rich in mercy and love.
Keep yourselves in God's love.
His love is priceless and unfailing.

Take refuge in the shadow of His wings.
In the end, faith, hope, and love will last.
The greatest of three is love.

February 8, 2025

Blessings for Families

Children who honour their father and mother are blessed.
Their days will be long in the land.
Parents who raise their children in the right way are blessed.
They will not leave the right path when they grow old.

Children are God's heritage given to parents.
They are like arrows in the hands of a warrior.
They will give praise to an excellent mother.

The man who has them is blessed, and his quiver is full.
They will be honoured even when they are faced with people against them.
Victory is on their side.

February 18, 2025

Blessings for Families (Continued)

Those who take care of their family and relatives are rewarded.

It is right for us to manage our house and care for God's people.

Love is always with them wherever they go and in all that they do.

Wives should treat their husband as the head.

And men should love their wives as themselves.

Children must obey their parents.

Forgiveness is powerful and brings healing to the soul.

Pleasant families bloom and grow closer together.

Joy is their strength and laughter, their medicine.

February 2025

Blessings for Families (Continued)

The father must manage his own family well and that his children obey him.
He must have respect and be worthy in his ways.
Then a wife can submit to her husband without opposition and fear.

Children should who obey their parents will receive their reward.
Families should honour the Lord and worship Him alone.
Give generously and you will receive generously in return.

Wear on God's full armour to protect yourselves.
Resist the devil and he will leave you.
Fathers must love their wife and their children.

February 18, 2025

Blessings for Families (Continued)

Be a light and guide to them, but don't anger them to hate you.
The man is the model for his family.
The wife is the one who loves and nurtures the children.
When they do right, then they will rule in the land.

A husband and wife are to be fruitful and increase in number.
They are to rule and reign righteously for the Lord.
They have become united.
Then God will give you the promised land.

February 2025

Blessings for Families (Continued)

Those who are upright will care for others.
Even the animals will have food to eat.
A noble wife is a husband's crown.
A virtuous woman is an excellent reward and rare to find.

Serve the Lord always and have your family serve Him too.
A son that is wise is a joy to his father.
A father should give instruction, and a mother teaches.
Praise the Lord with your soul, mind, and body.
Always remember and think of Him in always.
Do not forget His word and His promises.
It will keep your soul in the times of trouble.

February 2025

Blessings for Families (Continued)

Things will go well with you.
The righteous will bear much fruit.
They are a tree of life, and it is wise to save lives.
God rewards those who obey Him.
And rich will be the rewards of those who always do His will.

Remember the Lord and all His goodness.
Remember His excellent ways and His faithfulness.
Keep thanking Him and holding onto His truths.
Do not give up on prophecies, but fight the spiritual warfare for them to happen.

February 18, 2025

Blessings for Families (Continued)

Keep obeying the Lord's instructions and you will have everything that He promised.
He will do what He has promised if you don't give up.
Keep the faith and believe you have them already.
And they will be yours.

February 18, 2025

God of Mercies

God's mercies are new every morning.
He is the one that never changes.
He has plenty of mercy beyond your imagination.
It will never run dry.

Remember your days belong to the Lord.
Appoint each day for God's purpose and plan.
Command each day for His plan.
That you would have joy and have His glory.

The mercies of God last forever.
They are with you always.
Give praise for His mercies.
Give praise for His goodness.

February 25, 2025

God of Mercies (Continued)

The Blessing is a great.
The Blessing is more than enough.
The Blessing lasts forever. Amen.

The Lord is your answer every day.
He keeps you in His ways.
Every second is in His hand.
He is always righteous and always good.

February 25, 2025

God's Government Rule

The Lord rules the nations.
He is the judge of the whole earth.
Every man and woman are under His authority.

From the kings of the earth and the nations,
God is above them all.
He decides who will sit on the throne.

He allows evil to rule for a season.
Then judgment comes to them who do evil.
Their days are numbered, and all that they have will be taken away.

Greed and power blinds evil rulers.
They seek for money and control.
Others thirst for knowledge and wisdom.
God is above them all.

February 28, 2025

Government Rule (Continued)

The Lord is still in control and knows and sees everything they do.
Nothing is hidden from Him.
The wicked will last for a short time, and they will be no more.
The righteous will live forever in the Lord.

The Lord sits on the throne and gives authority and power to His people.
They rule and reign on the earth.
Those who seek the Lord will find wisdom, knowledge, and understanding.
They will be and be grateful.

February 25, 2025

Government Rule (Continued)

God's ways are higher than our ways.
It seems foolish to man.
The ways of the world are worthless in His eyes.
Man's wisdom is small before Him.

The righteous will enjoy days of blessing, honour, and glory.
Power and strength will be theirs.
The Lord is their shield and strong tower.
He is their very great reward.

The righteous will have victory in all that they do.
They will stand firm and strong.
Favour follows them everywhere they go.
Give thanks and praise. Amen.

February 25, 2025

Victory in the Lord

The Lord instructs, and He anoints.
The Lord gives His people victory over the enemy.
He gives them instructions and ideas.

Visions, dreams, signs, and wonders
to those who are His.
And they will hear the Lord and know Him by name.
When He calls, they will find Him.

The Lord is faithful to His righteous.
He will never leave them in want.
They will find favour and have a good name.

The Lord raises and His puts down.
He promotes those who are righteous.
And casts down those who are wicked.

March 8, 2025

Victory in the Lord (Continued)

The righteous will arise, and the wicked will fall.
Do not grow weary or tired.
Do not fear, for the Lord is here, and He is near.

The Lord will give you joy in times of want.
There, you will find strength.
In Him is the answer to all of your needs.

Trust in Him and He will not fail you.
Though the righteous may fall.
The Lord will raise them up again.

They will be glad all their days.
And the Lord will give their enemies into their hands.
Give thanks and praise!

March 8, 2025

Know the goodness of the Lord!

Thank you, Lord, for each day.
Thank you for each hour that I pray.
Thank you for keeping me away,
From the devil in every way.

Lord, you are always there for me.
Even when I can't see.
How God is working for me.

But I know that you will surely show,
So, all the world will know.
The greatness of the Lord
Is always said in His Word.

March 17, 2025

Know the goodness of the Lord! (Continued)

You can trust and obey as there is no other way.
To be happy in Jesus, but to trust and obey.
He will give you the strength to say.
The Lord has made a way!

March 17, 2025

God's faithful

The Lord is faithful to those who are His.
He keeps His promises all the time.
The righteous will reign and the wicked will fall.

God is head over all.
He lifts the humble
And puts down the proud.

He makes Himself known to all.
The Lord is awesome.
The Lord is great.

The Lord hides His face,
So that His people will seek and find Him.
He shows mysteries for kings to find.

March 18, 2025

Jesus' Fragrance

What is the smell of the beloved?
He is like spikenard and saffron.
His scent is also calamus and cinnamon.

The love of my soul is like the trees of frankincense,
He is like myrrh and aloes.
And you will also find the smell of chief spices.

My beloved is like a fountain in a garden.
He is a well of living waters and flowing streams.
And His garden is full of the best choice fruits.

My beloved's garden is full and has plenty.
It is like Lebanon.
Beautiful, healthy, and strong.
The Lord has blessed and has more than enough.

March 18, 2025

The Lord remembers

The Lord remembers the faithful and the just.
He will not hide His face from them when they call.
He has heard their prayers and will answer them.

The Lord loves justice and righteousness.
Wicked men, He will put them down.
He will remove them from their place.

Justice will be done, and freedom will come.
He doesn't forget the covenant that He made.
The Lord remembers all that He has said.

He changes times and seasons.
He makes paths straight in the wilderness.
Those who belong to the Lord will rejoice.

March 28, 2025

The Lord remembers (Continued)

They will give thanks and praise to the Lord.
Their mouth will continue to bring honour and glory to Him.
They will not remember the evil days anymore.

The Lord brought His people out of Egypt.
They went into the wilderness, and after years have passed.
They went into the Promised Land.

If they had obeyed the Lord, they would have gone in years before.
The Lord is not late in His coming.
He knows the perfect time for everything.

March 28, 2025

The Lord remembers (Continued)

Men are flesh and must put to death the things of the flesh.
When the flesh has lost its strength.
The Lord will bless and reward.

The flesh cannot inherit the blessings of God.
Therefore, we must deny ourselves and let Christ live in us.
He must be greater, and we must be lesser.

March 28, 2025

Passover Lamb

Our Passover Lamb who came to save man.
Christ has paid the price for us.
Upon the cross, He gave us freedom from our sins.

Through His blood, we are made clean.
He emptied Himself to give us everything.
The Great I Am, that became the Son of Man.

It is God's plan that He should be crushed.
He took all the pain to give us health.
All sickness and disease nailed on the cross.

Remember on this day, for this is God's way.
Give thanks and praise to His great name.
He will finish what He started from the beginning to the end.

April 8, 2025

Passover Lamb (Continued)

A new covenant was made on Passover Day.
A Holy Communion that He shares with us.
The promise as a spotless bride that He will take with Him.

Forever we will worship Him, the Lamb of God.
The Bread of Life, who gave us life.
The Healer, Provider, the Resurrected One

Betrayed by one of His own, yet he was not alone.
For God is with Him and the Holy Spirit.
He overcame, rose from the grave, and now sits on the throne.

April 8, 2025

Resurrection

Jesus has risen out of the grave.
He is risen! He is risen!
No power can keep Him there.

The Holy One has overcome it all.
He defeated the devil and took back the keys
That Adam and Eve gave up.

Jesus has made the captives free.
The strips on His back
Has paid the price for our sins.

April 14, 2025

Resurrection (Continued)

Jesus arose with life and healing.
He gave us victory.
Hallelujah! Hallelujah! to the Lamb of God!

He took back the keys that the devil stole.
Now we have power and authority.
We overcome our enemy through the Son of God.

Praise the Lord of the life that He gave.
In Him, we are purified.
A new creation and sealed forever.

April 14, 2025

First Fruits

Come before the Lord.
Honour Him with your wealth
And the fruit fruits of all your crops.

Then your barns will be filled to overflowing
And He will fill your vats to overflow with new wine.
The Lord has plenty and is rich and gracious.

Those who trust and obey will receive.
He will give more than enough to them.
And they will have no lack.

April 20, 2025

First Fruits (Continued)

Give the best to the Lord
and the first of all you have.
The best of your time and your talents.
The best of your food and finances.

Everything is for the Lord and
He will multiply back to you.
You will have more than enough.
He is a mighty and faithful God.

Give joyfully to the Lord and with a grateful heart.
And He will give you more than enough.
Rejoice and give thanks to the Lord.

April 20, 2025

First Fruits (Continued)

He is truly worthy of praise.
He gave us His best in everything.
Give honour and glory to the Lord.

Jesus is the first fruits of many brethren.
He has given us everything.
Blessings beyond our imagination.

Eternal life and His covenant.
He goes before us and will return for us.
To take us into heaven.

April 20, 2025

Righteous Government

The Lord appoints authorities, powers, and rulers.
That they may judge and rule on the earth justly.
That they would obey the laws of the Lord.

To show mercy to those
who should be shown mercy.
To judge the crimes of those who do wrong.
Make right the wrongs that are done.

That they spend the money wisely
in the right places.
Give to the Lord's people and to honour God.
Uphold righteousness and justice in the land.

To keep the people safe from their enemies.
To make peace with the countries around them.
Receive help when they need it.

April 26, 2025

Righteous Government (Continued)

To give to the poor
and care for the orphans and the widows.
That people pay their dues
and respect those above them.
To put the Lord first above all and follow His ways.

To show respect, mercy, and compassion to others.
To fund schools and communities to educate
and help the next generation.
Give programs and places for people to enjoy.

To provide the basics needs for living
and create jobs.
To make sure that houses
and buildings are fit for people to live in.
To provide services that people will need
to make their lives better.

April 26, 2025

Righteous Government (Continued)

A government that prays
and keeps their eyes on the Lord is blessed.
One who acknowledges God
and puts Him first is favoured.
One that rules with God's wisdom is exalted.

They shall be protected and will overcome all evil.
There will be peace in the land and joy overflowing.
The land will have plenty and multiply.

April 26, 2025

Mothers

Blessed is those who love the Lord.
Those who find strength and wisdom in Him.
They will never fail or lose hope.

The Lord is gracious and
merciful to all those who love Him.
He honours mothers and rewards them.
Blessed are those who honour the Lord
and who lives in the right way.

They will be the head and not the tail.
They will have plenty and not want.
They will overcome and do well all their days.

May 8, 2025

Mothers (Continued)

Long life comes to them and goodness
and mercy follows them.
Favour, grace, and blessing is theirs.
Peace, protection, and gifts are theirs.

A mother that is wise will build up her house.
She will raise her children to follow the Lord.
She loves the Lord and puts Him above all.

Strength belongs to her and she will bring comfort
to those around her.
Love will grow in her life and people will praise her.
All the works of her hands are blessed.

May 8, 2025

Mothers (Continued)

She is faithful in all that she does.
A godly mother who puts God first will always win.
She knows how to pray and worship the Lord.

When trouble comes, she knows what to do.
She trusts in the Lord and finds help in Him.
She runs from evil and is saved from danger.

Her husband will praise her and speak well of her.
She speaks well of others
and knows how to hold her tongue.
She knows how to build and encourage others.

May 8, 2025

Mothers (Continued)

A mother that fears the Lord is valuable
and precious.
There is none like her,
and she blooms even in times of difficulty.
She will stay strong and help her family overcome.

May 8, 2025

Families

Families are a blessing from the Lord.
He gives wisdom to the righteous.
The Lord keeps them on the narrow path.

He will stop the rage when it comes.
The Lord is faithful and just.
And He keeps the land of the righteous safe.

Families that are united are blessed by the Lord.
They will stand strong against the enemy.
They will never give up.

The Lord is gracious and merciful to the righteous.
He keeps them from evil and cares for them.
They will have no lack.

May 18, 2025

Families (Continued)

They will be the head and not the tail.
They will be above and not beneath.
The Lord will be their great reward.

He gives them more than enough.
No weapon formed against them will prosper.
Protection, and, peace, and honour belong to them.

They valulable in God's sight.
There is nother other like it.
Jesus makes a way for them.

May 18, 2025

God's chosen times and seasons

There are set times and seasons for everything.
The Lord controls them all.
He gives man a destiny on the earth to complete.

In God's time, all things are made new.
In His season, all things are made perfect.
Open doors happen, and old doors are closed.

Changes come, and old things go.
Know the times and seasons of the Lord.
Follow His ways and step through.

May 28, 2025

God's chosen times and seasons (Continued)

Do not miss the time of the Lord.
Blessings, favour, and plenty for you.
Jumping from one time to another.

The Lord will bring you through.
He will bring you to a new
and higher place than before.
Great things are to come
that are better than before.

May 28, 2025

Holy Spirit

Holy Spirit, mighty and strong.
Great in power and authority.
He shakes the nations and awakens hearts.

He is the Healer, Comforter, and Restorer.
Our Guide and Counselor, Protector and Teacher.
Holy and pure, and gentle.

Holy Spirit is a burning fire.
He is the light and like a mighty wind.
Quiet and patient.

Faster than lightning and wonderful.
He breaks down walls and mends hearts.
He reveals truth and satisfies the hungry and thirsty.

June 8, 2025

Holy Spirit (Continued)

Great are the gifts of the Holy Spirit.
Apostle, prophet, evangelist, pastor, and teacher.
Miracles, signs and wonders, tongues, and administration.

Revelation, understanding, prophecy, and more.
The seven-fold spirit of God:
The spirit of wisdom and understanding beyond us,
God's counsel and might and spirit of knowledge.
And He is the spirit of the fear of God.

He is everything that we need.
Holy Spirit shows us Jesus.
He tells us what to do every day.

June 8, 2025

Holy Spirit (Continued)

Just listen to the Holy Spirit and all will go well with you.
Though the enemy will fight you.
You will never give in but always win.

June 8, 2025

Overcoming loss

The Lord is our Comforter.
He is our refuge even in times of sadness.
We will find strength in the Lord always.

The Lord is our comfort and help.
He will always make a way for us.
Worry and fear must leave.

The Lord brings hope and peace.
He makes the mind still and quiet.
He gives joy in times of challenge.

June 18, 2025

Overcoming loss (Continued)

Remember the Lord and His goodness.
Remember the good things
that your loved ones have done.
Commit them to the Lord.

The Lord gives wisdom and guides your way.
He will not leave you lonely.
He will direct your path.

The Lord reunites families together.
He heals the broken hearts.
He gives new life to dead things.
The Lord takes away the pain.
There will no longer be any heart aches.
He creates fresh memories for you.

June 18, 2025

Canada

Canada be blessed
That the Lord rules from sea to sea
From the River to the ends of the earth
And that His glory, rule, and kingship be known
through you.

A peaceful land so strong and free.
Let your sons and daughters rejoice in you.
That your leaves bring healing to the nations.
And your bread basket feeds many.

A land of hope to all.
Rich in grace and mercy.
Blessed with shining waters and shining skies.

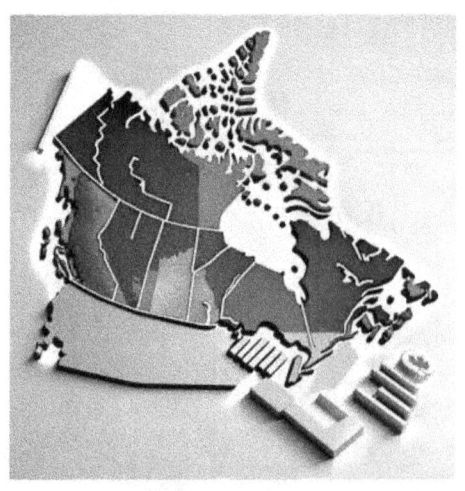

June 28, 2025

Canada (Continued)

A once humble land
That prayed to God in olden days.
Return sons and daughters to your beloved king.
Be strong and humble in prayer once again.

Let the king of glory come in.
That He would rule this land from west to east.
Awaken hearts and revive this land.

A land of maples and pine.
And blessed rivers flow.
A beloved native land.

June 28, 2025

Canada Arise

Awaken the ancient wells, forgotten over time.
Faithful sons and daughters arise
From the call of God.
Every prayer is heard.

Keeper of the universe, watch over our land.
Canada hold fast to His promises.
A day is coming for Canada to rise.

Nations will see the glory of the Lord.
Kings of the earth rejoice and be glad.
Finances will come and the wicked are judged.

A special purpose to honour the Lord.
Every eye will see and know the Lord.
He is God and there is no other.

June 28, 2025

Canada's Destiny

A land with beauty and a broad domain.
A light of hope to those who come.
Northern lights fill your skies.

Faithful ones stand firm in you.
They give praise to the one that's true.
Daily living lives for His good news.

In you, there is no lack.
From dominion to dominion.
There will be no end.

When the time comes, the Maker will be glad.
The faithful have done their part like He has said.
Be blessed Canada and shine for all to see.

June 29, 2025

Canada's Destiny (Continued)

Set apart for a glorious purpose.
Not to become part of another.
United, we stand and raise our hand to the Lord.

Bringing healing to many people.
At the Lord's command, miracles, signs, and wonders happen.
Nations are fed His Word.

And the glory of the Lord fills the earth,
As the waters fill the seas.
Truth and justice shall flow, and the land will produce its yield.

June 29, 2025

Canada's Destiny (Continued)

Rich rivers flow and blessings overtake His people.
Finances, prosperity, and wealth are in their hands.
Glory and honour belong to the Lord.

Supreme Ruler over this land.
Exalted are the humble
And the lowly who trust in you.
Blessed with a great and everlasting reward.

Seeking the better day to come.
Knowing His battle has been won.
He will take them away forever.

June 29 2025

Canada's Destiny (Continued)

Canada shall arise.
Fire of revival will fill its land.
Holy Spirit, we welcome you.

Make your presence known
And dwell among your people.
Let the nations know you are real.
Let the earth shake at sound of His voice.

Let the ancient wells revive.
The greatest revival will come.
It will boil over like a hot melting pot.
A volcano of molten lava that covers everything.

June 29 2025

Canada's Destiny (Continued)

No impure thing can live.
Only those with pure hearts
Who love the Lord will survive it.
And brings them strength and courage.

And they will do great things than before.
The earth shall know that there is a king.
A ruler who reigns supreme above all.

No matter can tell Him what to do.
For He has made His mind.
He will fulfill everything He has said.

June 29, 2025

Canada's Destiny (Continued)

He rules with justice and knows no defeat.
With his rod, He will judge
And make war against the nations.
Those who hate Him, He will destroy.

Those who love Him, He will save and bless greatly.
No man can stand in His presence
Except those with the Son of God.
He will hear them and answer them.

To the wicked He will not listen.
He pays no attention except to judge them
For the evil they have done.
For those who do not repent,
He will not show mercy.

June 29, 2025

Happy Birthday Canada

Happy Birthday Canada!
May you continue to remember the Lord.
And that your land will yield great harvests.

That many souls be turned from evil.
And become humble in prayer.
Blessed are your borders, streams, rivers, and seas.
Your coasts and ancient wells be wide and free.

Your northern skies stay beautiful
in the day and the night.
Shining brightly always for the Lord's delight.
May joy fills your cities, towns, and rural grounds.

July 1, 2025

Happy Birthday Canada (Continued)

Rich in resources and blessings.
A land of peace and hope.
Holy ones will rise from you
to take dominion over the land.

The Lord is your glorious reward,
who watches over you.
Remember your history O Canada.
Remember your destiny, for you have been chosen
for a special call.

July 1, 2025

Happy Birthday Canada (Continued)

Set apart from America,
never to be one land with them.
Canada, your leaves are for healing.
The Lord has provided for you and through you.

Many people will hear and obey the call.
They will do as the Lord has said.
He has not forgotten you but has kept you.

When the time is right, you will arise and shine.
Your light will go forth and many will be changed.
You are beloved by the Lord.

July 1, 2025

Happy Birthday Canada (Continued)

He has not forgotten His promise.
He will do it in His time.
Just wait and obey His commands.

Listen to the Holy Spirit.
He will lead you and guide you what to do.
Stay faithful to the Lord even to the end.

July 1, 2025

A Word for Canada

A trumpet for Canada will rise.
A man after God's own heart.
He will stand for Canada and Israel.

He will bring revival to this land
and he will bring the greatest prosperity
that this land has ever known.
Get ready, get ready Canada for your time is near.

The Lord is coming with a mighty hand
to bless those who are His.
He will judge the wicked.
Many families will come to know the Lord
in this time.

July 5, 2025

Power of the tongue

Words of faith are powerful.
They divide every wicked thing.
Breakthroughs, miracles, signs, and wonders
Coming from the righteous through Jesus.

Power to overcome and to break through.
Power and authority in your mouth.
Blessings instead of cursing.

Faith instead of doubt.
Rejoice in the Lord and be glad.
He opens doors that no man can shut.
He closes the door that no man can open.

July 8, 2025

Power of the tongue (Continued)

Be changed in your mind, soul, and body.
Worship and praise the Lord always.
Do not speak evil with your mouth,
But speak words that bring blessing.

By God's Word, we overcome.
No weapon formed against us will prosper.
We are the head and not the tail.
We have success in all that we do.

Favour, grace, and mercy follow us always.
Doors open up for us.
Victory is ours.

July 8, 2025

Miracles

Dormant inside, a fire is waiting to arise.
Then hope comes and awakens.
Joy revives life.

Excitement like never before.
A passion and grace shine through.
Favour beyond compare and peace like a river.

Promises yet to be fulfilled but not forgotten.
Faith restored and doors open.
The righteous are blessed and give God praise.

Miracles happen, signs and wonders.
The truth is revealed, and the people's hearts yield.
The sick are healed, and the lame walk.
The deaf hear and the mute speak.

July 18, 2025

Miracles (Continued)

The time has come for the redeemed to break free.
The trumpets sound and the people rejoice.
Revival is here, and the people draw near.

The Lord is here in their midst.
He comes with His glory and strength.
The Holy Spirit comes with power and might.
The captives are set free.

Disappointments are removed.
Sadness removed.
Anger uprooted.

July 18, 2025

Miracles (Continued)

God, the miracle worker.
He makes things work for me.
Miracles in the unseen and miracles that we see.

The miracle is working for you and me.
Faithful God who never sleeps day or night.
He performs miracles both day and night.

July 18, 2025

In Jesus Name

In Jesus' name, I can move the mountains.
In your name, I will not be afraid.
No weapon formed against me shall stand.

In the power of your name.
I am protected and not ashamed.
You rise high above.
I am shielded in your love.

In Jesus' name, I have the victory.
The enemy has to flee.
He has no hold on me.

July 28, 2025

In Jesus Name (Continued)

In Jesus' name, I trample the young lion
and serpent.
I will soar eagle's wings.
In the power of your name
Forever I am changed.

In Jesus' name, angels come to help me.
They defeat the enemy.
And he is at my feet.

In Jesus' name, I have all authority
To command the enemy
To return everything he stole from me sevenfold.

July 28, 2025

In Jesus Name (Continued)

In Jesus' name, I rule and reign.
No enemy can claim anything from me.
I stand righteous before the throne of God.
He has bought me with His love.

Forever I am free, because Jesus Christ lives in me.
One day, He will come to take me up above.
Forever we will reign, and He will never change.

In Jesus' name, He has won the victory.
The end draws near, but I will not fear.
For the Lord God is on my side.

In His glory, He will rise.
The enemy is defeated.
Forever judged for eternity.
Forever God's kingdom rules for eternity

July 28, 2025

God's Promises

In you, Lord, I believe in miracles.
In Jesus' name, I am more than a conqueror.
In the mighty name of Jesus, I can move the mountains.

Your name has power, your name has life.
Breaking every stronghold in my life.
Your name is above every name.

In Jesus' name, there is healing.
The mute speak; the lame can walk.
The blind can see, and the dead are raised to life.

August 4, 2025

God's Promises (Continued)

By the blood of Jesus, I am free.
No weapon formed against me will prosper.
Every tongue is condemned.

No judgment can stand against me.
Every lie of the enemy is destroyed.
Jesus has given me the kingdom and the authority.

All power, dominion, and glory belong to the Lord.
Jesus has given me the keys.
I take back my authority in Jesus' name.
I bind the work of the enemy
And I call for God's plan in my life.
Every prayer is a weapon of victory.

August 4, 2025

God's Promises (Continued)

We prophesy by the Holy Spirit.
The word of truth is changing our situation
To make way for God's plan.

And all will see God's glory.
People will arise and be surprised.
The Lord's blessings will overflow.

The Great Awakening comes and stirs up a revival.
A massive harvest and Christ's return draw near.
Then the number of the Gentiles is now fulfilled.

The bride will be taken away.
The great day of the Lord will come.
All will fear and know the Lord is God.

August 4, 2025

Transition

In a time of transition, hold on to your faith.
Do not let circumstances tell you lies
That God has heard your prayers.

The devil will tell you lies.
To make you deny God's promises.
But through Jesus, you have won and overcome.

God sits on the throne, so you are not alone.
Take your authority and arise.
Give the devil a surprise.

Don't let him see fear.
Know that God is near.
He is your victor here.

August 8, 2025

Transition (Continued)

You don't give up.
Your reward will come.
Greater than what you know.

Nothing is impossible for God.
He is always on your side.
He will lift you high above the enemy.

Take a walk of faith.
Dare to believe that God is who He says He is.
He can't lie and won't deny those who are His.

August 8, 2025

Transition (Continued)

The truth is revealed and sealed
In the hearts of those who believe.
The mark of the Lord by the blood of the Lamb.

He has kept us safe.
The enemy can't win
And we will see God's great glory.
As He comes to show Himself to all.

Wait on the Lord, and you will have your reward.
Greater than what you can believe.
God's blessing will pour and be so much more.
Than what you think you will receive.

August 8, 2025

God's Abundance

God owns cattle on a thousand hills.
He has greatness beyond our understanding.
Riches and wealth beyond our sight.

God's name is not like others.
He is faithful and abundant in every way.
He clothes the lilies and feeds the birds.

There is no lack in God's kingdom.
The Lord has secrets to share.
He tells it to His holy ones.

August 8, 2025

God's Abundance (Continued)

Those who love the Lord will be blessed.
They will be the head and not the tail
And above and not beneath.

They will always have plenty.
He is the Lord of more than enough.
And they will be satisfied in Him.

August 8, 2025

Waiting for the Promises of God

Waiting for the Promises of God
It is a test for you and me
But puts our spirit at peace.

The flesh can't have what God wants for us.
The self must be denied.
God can't lie but only speaks the truth in love.

The devil steals and lies to make us give.
The Lord is wise and gives us a surprise.
We won't give up because, through Jesus Christ, we have already won.

August 15, 2025

Waiting for the Promises of God (Continued)

Have faith in the Lord.
He is your great reward and in Him is abundance.
The devil is defeated.

Hold fast to His promises.
They all you need.
The Lord is more than enough.

His wealth, riches, and honour are great.
In Him, you will overflow.
Help others in need and show them the way to go.
Fast and pray to know the way.
God has given us the authority
Through Christ Jesus the Son of God and Man.

August 15, 2025

Waiting for the Promises of God (Continued)

Jesus Christ, the King of Glory.
He rules in everything.
Through Him all things are made right.

A time is coming and will soon be here.
People will know the Lord.
A mighty harvest of souls.

The people will rush in.
People with needs, and then they will see
The goodness of the Lord.

August 15, 2025

God of Armies

A sound is heard like a great multitude.
Like Nations that gather together.
The Lord Almighty and his army.

His people are mighty warriors.
Full of the armour of God, they stand against the devil.
No weapon can form against them.

Announce to the nations and prepare for war.
Let the warriors rise to fight.
The Lord of the breakthrough is here.

August 18, 2025

God of Armies (Continued)

Rejoice in the Lord always.
Praise the Lord, your Rock.
He trains our hands for war and fingers for battle.

The Lord commands His angels.
To guard us in all our ways.
He lifts us with His hands.

He protects the righteous from evil.
The Lord's angel armies fight on behalf of His people.

The people raise the banner of Righteousness.
The people of God are united.
The Lord Jesus is their King.
With a two-edged sword, He destroys the enemy.

August 18, 2025

God of Armies (Continued)

There are more angels with us than the enemy.
Speak God's command, and they will go forth.
The Lord has given His people the authority.

God's people have dominion over the earth.
The enemy is defeated under their feet.
The devil and his angels will be thrown into the lake of fire.

Praise the God in the highest.
Worship before His throne.
Give thanks for all He has done.

August 18, 2025

Spiritual Warfare

Take your authority in Jesus.
The weapons of our God
The divine power to break strongholds.

We destroy arguments
And everything that comes
against the knowledge of God.
We take captive every thought
that comes against Christ.

We put on God's armour
And fight against rulers and authorities,
Against cosmic powers and spiritual forces of evil
In the heavenly places.

August 28, 2025

Spiritual Warfare (Continued)

We stand firm on God's Word.
The sword of the Spirit is in our hands.
We wage war against the enemy.

By the blood of Jesus, we overcome.
We submit ourselves before our God
And resist the devil, and he flees from us.

We dwell in the shelter of the Most High
And abide in the shadow of the Almighty.
The Lord is our refuge and fortress.

August 28, 2025

Spiritual Warfare (Continued)

The Lord is our deliverer.
He makes us clean from all sin.
He is faithful and just.

The Lord protects us from the enemy.
He lifts us up above the enemy.
We tread on serpents and scorpions.

Our enemies are defeated.
By our faith, we overcome the world.
Every tongue against us is silenced.

The Lord gives us favour and honour.
He raises us high above.
He blesses us with more than enough.

August 28, 2025

Power of the mouth

Open your mouth to give thanks and praise to our God, for He is worthy.
He is highly exalted in all the earth.
Therefore, let your mouth give glory and honour to His name.

The Lord is mighty in power and authority.
Just as you praise, on your tongue, speak the truth in love.
Let out a joyful sound.

Do not give up when things are hard.
Speak in faith and hold fast to the Lord.
Exalt His name and continue to speak His Word.

September 1, 2025

Power of the mouth

Hold onto His promises.
Hold your tongue from evil.
Speak life and blessing.

Guard your heart.
Do not listen to the wicked.
Their words are toxic to your ears.

Wisdom is found among the godly.
They keep their heart pure.
It brings health to your body, soul, and mind.

The Lord opens the door and gates for His people.
With shouts of victory, they overcome.
Laugh in the Lord and believe the Lord.

September 1, 2025

Power of the mouth

Nothing is impossible for the Lord.
Even when evil strikes against you,
And when people cause you trouble.

Those who seek to annoy and make you angry.
The Lord will judge them all.
Keep silent before them.

As you rejoice and don't look at them
And don't think of them,
The Lord will open the way for you.

You will not see them anymore.
The Lord is just and loves the righteous.
He will not allow the wicked to win.

September 1, 2025

The Lord knows all

The Lord laughs over His enemies.
What is man in His eyes?
He is like a speck of dust made from clay
That the Lord breathed into.

Let the people understand.
He is above the nations.
The Lord sees everything that man does.

He knows every word before the man speaks.
Every hair on his head is counted.
Everything that he does and where he goes.
They are written in His book.

September 1, 2025

The Lord knows all (Continued)

The wicked are doomed for destruction.
The righteous are raised to glory.
The Lord knows all their ways.

All of man's plans are known to the Lord.
There is nothing hidden from Him.
The Lord's thoughts are higher than his thoughts.
His ways are higher than man's ways.

Yet the Lord takes delight in man.
He favours him and gives him everything,
That he needs for life and godliness.

September 1, 2025

The Lord knows all (Continued)

It is to complete God's plans and walk in His ways.
Do God's kingdom work and you will not lack.
Know His Word and live by it in faith.

In the Lord, there are mysteries.
Secrets to find out.
He shows them to the kings.

The Lord's laughter is healing and medicine
To a man's bones, his soul, and body.
It gives him peace of mind and joy in his heart.

September 1, 2025

Repentance and Jesus' Return

The Lord says:
If my people will humble themselves and pray,
I will hear from heaven and heal their land.
I will answer when they call.

When they turn from sin,
I will draw near and bless them.
Heaven will open, and I will pour on them.

They will be protected from the enemy.
They will be exalted.
They will overcome.

September 2, 2025

Repentance and Jesus' Return (Continued)

If my people will humble themselves,
Then I will hear from heaven and heal their land.
I will answer when they call.

As they seek my face, I will show myself to them.
As they hear my voice, I will speak to them.
As they obey my Word, I will reward them.

Then my presence will come.
The Holy Spirit will flow.
Miracles, signs, and wonders will happen.

People will be healed and saved.
Deliverance will happen.
Breakthroughs will increase.

September 2, 2025

Repentance and Jesus' Return (Continued)

Finances will grow.
The people will have success.
The nations will be changed.

Revival will come.
God's promises are fulfilled.
Jesus will return, and the bride will be taken.

Then the end will come.
A new heaven and earth will be created.
The Lord will reign forever. Amen.

September 2, 2025

Be Holy for the Lord is Holy

Be Holy for, the Lord is Holy.
Wash yourselves in the blood of the Lamb.
Repent of all your sins.

Pass by the outer court into the holy place.
Prepare yourself as a holy offering.
Let the Word of God speak to you.

Come before the Lord.
Wait in His presence.
Let the Holy Spirit work in you.

September 2, 2025

Be Holy for the Lord is Holy (Continued)

Walk and obey His Word as a daily offering.
Let the Lord fill you with the Holy Spirit.
He will restore, refresh, and revive your soul.

Put on the armour of God.
Speak His Word every day and pray.
Worship the Lord in all you do.

Keep the Lord in your heart and mind.
Let Him be first in everything you do.
Believe and receive all He has for you.

September 2, 2025

Rejoice in the Lord

Rejoice in the Lord.
First, blow a trumpet in Zion.
Then, let all the people fear the Lord.

Next, wake up and hear His voice.
The Lord is coming back for a pure and spotless bride.
He will come to the holy mountain.

Israel rejoices before your King.
He is coming soon on a white horse.
He will judge the nations.

September 3, 2025

Rejoice in the Lord (Continued)

The trumpets will be heard on the day of the Lord.
When He comes to take His bride away.
They will not be seen again.

Quickly repent, people of God before the Lord comes.
Seek His face and do His will, for your time is short.
You don't know when the Lord will come.

When the Lord returns, He will take those who are His.
Those who are waiting and ready.
They will be changed and taken quickly.

September 3, 2025

Rejoice in the Lord (Continued)

They will wear white robes.
They will live with the Lord forever.
In heaven, they will have a new home.

There will no longer be any weeping.
No fear or worry.
No pain, lack, or anger.

The Lord is their husband, and they are His bride.
They will forget the past
And live in mansions forever.

September 3, 2025

Breakthrough

The Lord is the God of breakthroughs.
He makes a way where there seems to be no way.
Rivers in the desert and a highway in the wilderness.

Your land will no longer be like Buelah.
You will be married and be like Hephzibah.
He makes you rich with plenty.

The dry places will become springs of water.
Your valleys will become filled.
The Lord is the God of the harvest.

September 3, 2025

Breakthrough (Continued)

He will revive and restore you.
You will have peace, hope, health, and healing.
You will laugh in days to come.

The Lord delights in His people.
They will delight in the Lord.
They will be satisfied and overflow.

Things will become easy for you.
The doors and gates open up.
The blockages are removed.

September 3, 2025

Breakthrough (Continued)

As you repent and turn from your sin.
The Lord opens new doors again.
And the enemy has to leave.

You are now set free.
Now, you must bring glory to His name.
Seek His face and do His will
And it will be good for you.

September 3, 2025

Dismantling Strongholds

The Lord is the Lord of Hosts.
He breaks down strongholds.
He overturns evil plans.

The Lord gives victory to His people.
He gives authority and dominion to them.
They rise up and overcome.

Tear down the walls that stop you.
Do not give up, but fight to win.
The Word of God is your weapon.

September 4, 2025

Dismantling Strongholds (Continued)

Let praise come out of your mouth.
The Lord makes his enemies his footstool.
He levels the land, and no enemy will stand.

Those who stand against him will fall.
He destroys the wicked and ends their evil plans.
The righteous walks with ease.

The angels of the Lord surround His people.
They lift them up.
They protect them from their enemies.
Every prayer is a powerful weapon.
It makes every evil wall fall.
The narrow path is open to the righteous.

September 4, 2025

Dismantling Strongholds (Continued)

The Lord crushes the enemy.
The righteous tramples them
down under their feet.
They will soar on eagle's wings and not grow weary.

The Lord judges the evil for their ways.
He destroys their crops and empties their banks.
They will have nothing.

The wicked will be forgotten.
Their name will be removed
from the face of the earth.
The righteous will have honour
and be remembered.

September 4, 2025

Dismantling Strongholds (Continued)

The Lord sets the captives free.
He breaks their chains.
The righteous rejoice and are glad.

The devil is defeated,
and his lies will no longer be heard.
The righteous hear the voice of the Lord.
They are saved and succeed in all that they do.

The Lord has given His people authority.
They are anointed to rule and reign.
And the Lord is their provider.

September 4, 2025

Dismantling Strongholds (Continued)

They will not struggle in the days to come.
The Lord will take care of them all their days.
Many will come to know the Lord
And they will be saved.

When trouble comes,
The Lord makes a way for them.
He brings them out of danger
And gives them more than enough.

Miracles will happen for the righteous.
Blessings and favour will come.
The wicked will suffer loss and not overcome.

September 4, 2025

Rapture

In a twinkling of an eye, the people of God will be taken.
They will not be seen anymore.
Because the Lord has taken them.

They wear robes of white and have a new body.
A new name is given to them by the Lord.
They are sealed forever by His Spirit.

The day of the Lord comes quickly.
He will destroy the wicked.
Scorpions will attack them.

September 5, 2025

Rapture (Continued)

The false prophet and Antichrist will fall.
The demons are judged.
Satan is burned in the lake of fire forever.

The earth is judged, and the old heaven removed.
A new heaven and earth are created.
The Lord's people reign on it.

The kingdom of God is established.
His people reign and rule forever.
They will live in houses made for them.

September 5, 2025

Rapture (Continued)

The lion will rest with the Lamb.
There will no longer be sadness, sorrow, or pain.
The bride has a new body that lives forever.

The new Jerusalem shines forth.
She is adorned with gold.
Its doors are made of pearl.
The fountains of various gemstones.

The names of the apostles
And the tribes of Israel are written on her.
Her light is the Lord God Almighty.

September 5, 2025

Rapture (Continued)

New Jerusalem is beautiful.
She is like a bride to the Lamb of God.
Those who live in her borders are safe.

Heaven's gates are open to the bride.
She finds favour with her bridegroom.
She will be satisfied all the days of her life.

The Lord is faithful and just.
He remembers His promises and completes them.
He will never abandon His people.

September 5, 2025

Rapture (Continued)

Be ready for the Lord's return.
For you do not know what day is hour He will come.
You must stay close and obey Him while you wait.

The Lord has set the times and seasons.
Things are coming together.
He tells His prophets His plans.

He will make known to them the future.
The devil's time is short.
He knows it is coming to an end.

September 5, 2025

Rapture (Continued)

The Lord is working and will bring things to pass.
The end is coming, so be ready.
Share the gospel while you can.

Obey the Lord in all He tells you to do.
Do not allow your time to be lost
Be wise and know the season.

Do not give up, and the Lord will reward you.
Be confident to speak His Word.
Pray always and read His Word.

September 5, 2025

Rapture (Continued)

Claim His Promises.
Declare His protection over you.
Plead the blood.
Resist the devil and he will leave you.

September 5, 2025

Spiritual Gifts

The Lord has given everyone gifts, uniting us in purpose.
There is one body, made up of many members.
Each one has different gifts that we need.

There are gifts of prophecy.
Gifts of faith, miracles, signs, and wonders.
Gifts of teaching, works of ministry.

Gifts of exhortation.
The ability to give to others,
The ability to lead with diligence.

September 6, 2025

Spiritual Gifts (Continued)

Those who show mercy and are cheerful.
People who are dedicated and serve the Lord.
Rejoicing in hope, patient in difficulty,

Continuing always in prayer.
Distributing to the needs of saints,
Given to hospitality.

Bless those who persecute,
Bless and rejoice in the Lord.
Have the same mind in Christ.

September 6, 2025

Miracles

The people of Israel saw God's signs and wonders.
He made the Red Sea to allow dry land.
The people were chased by Pharaoh.

Pharaoh became no more.
He tried to capture God's people,
But he and his people failed.

The Lord was a pillar of fire at night and a cloud by day.
He split the sea for the children of Israel.
The people plundered the Egyptians.

September 6, 2025

Miracles (Continued)

The Lord is gracious and compassionate.
He is slow to anger and great in love.
The Lord is faithful to His people.
They will have great peace.

September 6, 2025

Blessings

Blessings from above.
The Lord gives abundantly.
More than enough.

He favours those who are His.
They receive all His goodness.
Mercy and breakthroughs come.

Open heaven to His people.
He opens the door nobody can shut.
He shuts a door that nobody can open.

September 8, 2025

Blessings (Continued)

Blessed are those who follow the Lord.
They will be blessed in all they do.
He opens up portals for them.

He will never leave them.
They will find green pasture.
They are blessed all their days.

September 8, 2025

The Lord answers

The Lord has heard my prayers.
He has answered.
Favour and blessing come to the righteous.

The wicked lose heart.
At the sound of the Lord's voice, they are judged,
yet the upright are glad.
They are judged.

The upright are glad.
The Lord has avenged His people and set them free.
He has set them free

SEPTEMBER 10, 2025

The Lord answers (Continued)

The Lord gives good things,
He gives the best to His people.
He gives them great success.

Do not forget the Lord.
He will remember His people.
They will never lose hope.

Ask for the open heavens.
Ask for the gates and portals to be opened,
Declare all God has for you.

September 10, 2025

The Lord answers (Continued)

Remember the Lord on the day of your birthday.
He will pour out more for you.
Then ever before.

Birthdays are important to the Lord.
They bring a breakthrough for you.
Celebrate them and ask for blessings.

Do not forget to celebrate your day,
The enemy seeks to rob you.
You must stand and fight.

September 10, 2025

Surprises

The Lord gives surprises.
We don't know when they will come.
They are more than one.

He gives more than you ask.
The righteous will receive more.
The Lord multiplies more than before.

Remember the Lord as your source.
He will keep you on course.
And surround you with angels.

September 11, 2025

Surprises (Continued)

You will not go astray.
And you will not look the other way,
When good things come.

Your future will be bright.
God is your light.
He controls both day and night.

There is a time and a season.
And a very good reason
When God doesn't give you all you want.

He knows what's best.
He will put you to the test.
And you will have rest,

September 11, 2025

Surprises (Continued)

Believe and receive.
All your rewards are there.
They will overflow like never before.

God is rich indeed,
So you will never have a need.
If you trust, obey.

Learn to hold back the flesh.
And you will not lack.
God will always watch your back.

September 11, 2025

Creation

Let the mountains, hills, and valleys rejoice,
At the sound of God's voice.
He makes the nations glad.

All creation waits for the sons of God,
To rise up and restore them.
They long to bring life and fruitfulness.

Awaken the ancient wells.
Let the earth rejoice.
All creation sings to the Lord.

September 12, 2025

Creation (Continued)

The oceans clap their waves.
The flowers bloom in season.
The animals also dance.

New birth happens.
He causes laughter.
The Lord clothes the flowers.

He made a covenant with man.
A rainbow in the sky,
As a reminder of His promise.

September 12, 2025

Creation (Continued)

The clouds give rain.
The plants are fed.
The sun shines its light.

The moon glows at night.
The stars shine in the sky.
All the planets spin on course.

The eagles soar in the sky.
The whales blow out water.
The dolphins play in the ocean.

September 12, 2025

Creation (Continued)

Creatures below hide in coral.
The unknown land stays hidden from view.
Places void of man.

The hyenas laugh in mischief.
The coyotes howl at night.
The owls hoot in the trees.

The cock crows in the morning.
The early man rises up.
The farmers work their land.

September 12, 2025

Creation (Continued)

The cows graze in the grass, enjoying the sun.
The sheep lie comfortably in the grass.
The shepherds watch the flock by day and night.

September 12, 2025

Suddenlies

The Lord is the God of suddenlies.
He makes things happen suddenly.
You may not know when and how.

Instead of worrying, place your trust in the Lord.
He will expedite things for you.
As you seek the Lord, you will see Him work things out on your behalf.

Hold onto His promises.
Hold fast to the Word of God.
Stand firm in faith for your prophecies.

September 15, 2025

Suddenlies (Continued)

The Lord makes miracles happen.
What is unseen today may soon be revealed before you.
The supernatural will make the way for you.

Follow the Lord in all you do.
Put Him first in your life.
Remember what He said and do His will.

September 15, 2025

Suddenlies (Continued)

The door will open up.
Favour will follow you everywhere you go.
Things will become easier, and your answers will come quickly.

It is the time and the season for miracles.
Anything is possible with God.
Do not doubt, but only believe and receive.

Blessings will come.
You will have more than enough.
Dreams will come true.

September 15, 2025

Spiritual Speed

The Lord is faster than lightning.
He moves quicker than the eye can see.
The Lord knows the perfect time.

He makes things happen in their perfect season.
All things are made beautiful.
There is a time for everything.

The Lord makes the righteous move swiftly.
He causes the enemy to slow down and fall.
The Holy Spirit is faster than the cheetah.

September 15, 2025

Spiritual Speed (Continued)

?The Lord will do things quickly for His children.
Those who have waited long.
There will no longer be a delay.

The time has come for a breakthrough to come.
The day will come when God will get all the glory.
The enemy will no longer have the fun.

The reward will come to the righteous.
The judgment will come to the wicked.
The righteous will have plenty.

September 15, 2025

Spiritual Speed (Continued)

The wicked will become empty.
The Lord will restore even more,
The people of God will pour out more.

Honour will come, and they have won.
Glory be to God in the Highest.
Forever He reigns in heaven and earth.

September 15, 2025

Celebrate

Celebrate God's promises.
Rejoice and be glad in the Lord.
Make music and sing praises.

The Lord is your reward.
He will give you great harvests.
Hold onto His Word.

Give thanks to the Lord always.
Know that He is good.
He will do what He has promised.

September 18, 2025

Celebrate (Continued)

You will have plenty
if the Lord is the apple of your eye.
Fix your eyes on Jesus.
Believe and receive by faith.

Know that you have what you asked for.
What God promised, believe you have it.
Walk each day knowing that God brings it to you.

The wicked will have nothing.
Even what they gain, they will lose.
Though they don't know it, their end is near.

September 18, 2025

Celebrate (Continued)

The righteous celebrate.
They will be thankful that the Lord answers them.
He gives them more than enough to bless others.

The Lord does good to those He loves.
He takes from those who despise him.
God is faithful to His people.

The wicked will be judged.
The righteous will be rewarded.
Jesus Christ will be praised forever.

September 18, 2025

Wealth and riches for the righteous

The Lord will reward the righteous.
A day will come when there will be plenty.
Many miracles will happen.

The Lord will take from the wicked.
He will give to the righteous more than enough.
The good news will reach the ends of the earth.

The wicked fall and lose all they saved.
Their place will be empty.
The righteous will be glad.

September 18, 2025

Wealth and riches for the righteous (Continued)

There may be crashes, but the Lord will restore.
The Lord will raise them up.
Many will become great.

The righteous will rise up.
Those who are pure in heart will see God.
They will be richly rewarded.

The godly will become rich.
The wicked will become poor.
The wicked will be no more.

September 18, 2025

Wealth and riches for the righteous (Continued)

At the hand of the Lord,
The wicked will fall.
At the hand of the Lord,
The righteous will rise.

The great harvests will come.
Watch and pray.
Listen and obey.
Do not go astray nor turn away from the Lord.

Keep a guard over your heart and your mouth.
Stay pure in heart.
Speak God's word from day to night.

September 18, 2025

Wealth and riches for the righteous (Continued)

Remember the Lord in all your ways.
Do not forget Him.
Seek the Lord always, and He will be found.

The Lord loves those who love Him.
He remembers them
and gives them a place to call home.
Riches and wealth are in their hands.

Thanksgiving and gratefulness
in their hearts and mouths.
They will stand firm in hard times
and will not give up.
They will overcome with ease in the days to come.

September 18, 2025

SALVATION PRAYER

God, I know I sinned against you. Forgive me for the wrong that I have done. I believe that Jesus Christ died on the cross for me. He rose from the grave after three days. I can have His long-lasting life. Come into my heart to be my Lord and Savior. I choose to turn away from my sins, and I choose to follow you. Lead me to walk with you. Keep me safe and teach me your ways. Stop every bad thing in my life that has an open door to hurt me. Close those doors. Holy Spirit, fill me now in Jesus' name. Amen.

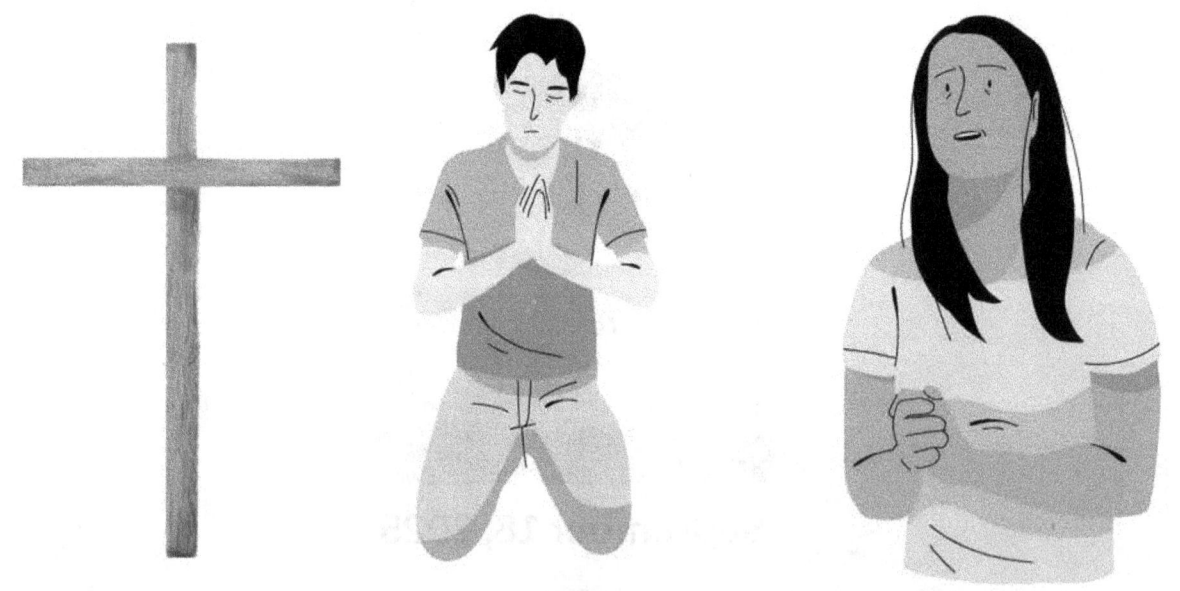

BAPTISM OF THE HOLY SPIRIT

Jesus, you are the one who fills me with Your Spirit. Come, Holy Spirit, and come into my life and fill me to overflow with Your presence. Come with your fire, too. Thank you for the gift of tongues in Jesus' name. Amen.

Open your mouth and let the words come out that God gives you. It will be words that you don't know what they mean. You can ask God what it means. You need to let Him talk through you every day to grow this gift.

He will bring you closer to God, and you will know Jesus more intimately. You will have power from God to do great things and know things.

PRAYER

Thank you, God, Jesus, and the Holy Spirit, for this collection of psalms and poems from your heart. Thank you for encouraging and bringing comfort, joy, peace, and more into my life. Draw me close to you and grant me wisdom, knowledge, and understanding. Keep me in your ways. I pray to be a vessel of honour and glory for you. Let your light shine through my life and each day to change me to become more like Jesus. Let my songs rise and be released in many lives and change them. Joy and passion rise. Let revival come in our nation. Bring back the awe of God in our hearts and leaders to have your heart in Jesus' name. Prepare me for your return, in Jesus' name. Amen.

MESSAGE FROM THE AUTHOR

My hope is that you have been encouraged by these psalms and poems, which are written from the heart. Lately, I have been prompted to produce warnings. These days, hackers have the technology to use Flipper Zero and steal all of your information stored on your digital devices. Do not connect to public Wi-Fi networks. Stay connected to dedicated secure networks. Do not share or store content online that is secure. Any device with an internet connection can be hacked into. They can take all your passwords, pins, etc. Storing to a phone is usually not ideal. Your phone should not be logged into OneDrive, Google Drive, etc, when on Wi-Fi. Use a VPN to protect yourself. Do not open strange emails, as they are phishing attempts. Scammers will increase in number. Protect your things by staying secure and upgrading all devices.

MESSAGE FROM THE AUTHOR

Stay away from opening emails, messages, or pop-ups that you don't know. Avoid charging your phone in public places. Hackers can replace your cable with a fake one to spy on you and steal all you have. They can also do the same with a lightbulb and your security camera. They can access through signals and networks in public places.

We have been warned many times that the Lord is coming soon. He is, and there are prophecies yet to be fulfilled before He returns. We have been warned of our wars, floods, market crashes, electricity will go out for a time, currency change, famine, pestilence, and more. Take courage and remember the Lord is first. If you remain in Him, you will be protected and go through all these and not be shaken. You will live through them and be prepared when they come.

REFERENCES

Biblegateway, NIV. N/A, https://www.biblegateway.com/

OTHER PRODUCTS

- Knowing God
- How to Hear God's Voice
- New Life in Jesus
- Loving Israel
- God's Gifts/Spiritual Talents
- Meeting God
- Word Power
- Fruit of the Spirit
- The Tabernacle
- Bride for Jesus
- A Life of Prayer
- Live Free
- Who am I in Jesus
- Walk in Love
- God's Favor
- Man of God
- Woman of God
- How to Use Money
- God's Wisdom
- Fasting
- See Jerusalem and Bethany
- First Fruit Offering
- Feast of Trumpets
- Day of Atonement
- Feast of Tabernacles
- Counting the Omer
- Festival of Lights
- Glory, Presence, and Holy Spirit
- Live in God's Presence
- How God Speaks
- Knowing Jesus
- Knowing Holy Spirit
- A Healthy Life and Healthy Life Work Book
- Smokey the Cat
- Passover Unleavened Bread
- Resurrection Life
- The Blessing
- Chelsea Learns Hebrew
- Give Thanks
- Thanksgiving
- Revival
- Jesus' Birth
- Proverbs 31 Woman
- Loving Jesus: Bride and Groom
- Colours in the Bible
- Breakthroughs
- Open Doors
- The Seven Spirits of God
- Numbers in the Bible

OTHER PRODUCTS

Aglee the Eagle
An Eagle's Life
ABC's of Faith
Angels
Chelsea Learns Numbers in Hebrew
Feast of Purim
A Royal Life
Chiinese New Year
Family Day
Family Blessings
Loving Jesus for Children
Worship
Pandas
Canada
Celia's Birthday
Animal Stories
Eagles

Coming soon

Fun in West Caribbean
Courtroom of God
Fun in Yellowknife
Windsor
Tecumseh

Puzzle Books

Biblical Puzzle Book Volume 1-5
Bible Puzzles for Young Children Book 1-3
Biblical Puzzle for Children Books 1-5
Chelsea's Bible Puzzles

Devotionals

31 Day Devotional

Inspirational/Other

Chelsea's Psalms and Poems
Your Daily Meal: Chelsea's Food Album
Chelsea's Psalms and Poems 2
Travel West Caribbean
Chelsea's Recipes

Coming soon

Travel Alberta
Chelsea's Psalms and Poems 4
Travel to Yellowknife
Chelsea's Psalms and Poems5
Travel Vancouver
Travel in Labrador

OTHER PRODUCTS

Teaching Series

How to Hear God's Voice Teaching Guide & Audio Book
Relationship with God, Jesus, Holy Spirit Guide
Knowing God, Jesus, Holy Spirit Guide & Audio Book
Flowing in the Prophetic

More books to come!

Teaching (Non-Sale on the website)

Purim
Passover
Resurrection

More books on Amazon, Kobo, and Barnes and Noble, and Smashwords.
https://chelseak532002550.wordpress.com/

OTHER PRODUCTS

More books on Amazon, Kobo, Barnes and Noble, and Smashwords.
https://www.amazon.com/author/chelseakong

Please leave a review to help the author continue to write more books to reach more readers. Thank you so much for your support.

Review!

About
CHELSEA KONG

She is a writer, creative arts and digital media artist, skilled administration, and certified PCP (Payroll Compliance Professional), and podcaster. Chelsea also served in a variety of roles, from audiovisual, photography, to assisting on the worship team, and ministry team. She also has a passion for families being united.

Chelsea has been a guest on Unity Live Radio, The Lady Tracey Show, and How to Live for Christ, and is highly recommended by a Proud Christian blog. She is also a guest blogger. A few of her books have been featured in YourAuthorHub, etc. She has a diploma in Hotel and Restaurant Management, Digital Media Arts, and Office Administration, and she is certified as a Payroll Compliance Professional, and experience working with children. Chelsea lives in Toronto, Canada. She mainly writes children's books, stories, bridal writing, poems, lyrics for songs, words of encouragement, blessings, prayers, and jokes. The author of How to Hear the Voice of God, the Bridal Collection, Knowing God, etc. She also has her own Bible Puzzle books and other inspired products. Her podcast channel is called Chelsea K on Anchor, Spotify, and iTunes.

Please check my website to find out more:
https://chelseak532002550.wordpress.com/

www.ingramcontent.com/pod-product-compliance
Lightning Source LLC
Chambersburg PA
CBHW080222170426
43192CB00015B/2723